PAUL EARL EUBANKS

LEARNING 2 WALK AGAIN

authorHOUSE®

AuthorHouse™
1663 Liberty Drive
Bloomington, IN 47403
www.authorhouse.com
Phone: 1 (800) 839-8640

Published by AuthorHouse 04/24/2018

ISBN: 978-1-5462-3939-0 (sc)
ISBN: 978-1-5462-3938-3 (hc)
ISBN: 978-1-5462-3937-6 (e)

Library of Congress Control Number: 2018904952

Print information available on the last page.

Scripture taken from The Holy Bible, King James Version. Public Domain

CONTENTS

To the bread of life, my Alpha and Omega, the creator of everything that dwells in me. I honor You and willingly yield my life unto You and surrender all that I am unto You. I thank You for the vessel that You allowed me to enter into this world through, my mother Ruth Francis Eubanks. Because of every seed that You have planted in her and she has instilled in me, I am able to walk my path and my calling with integrity. I am honored to bear the fruit of wisdom, knowledge, and courage from her. My prayer is and will always be for You to use me for Your glory. Allow me to be an example and to be effective in my living for the youth that will follow me as a light out of darkness.

To my babies Azariah Antwon Scott, Uzziah Johnson, Ryan Milliner, Elijah David Milliner, Cayden Dexter, and my baby girl Princess Zoey Oduagu (the leader of the pack). I pray that each of you grow into your purposed life knowing your worth, trusting in God daily, and never allowing anyone to order your steps for you but God. I pray that you lead by example and never be followers, and that you take life one step at a time as you boldly cross over into your calling and into your purposed life that God has manifested for each of you.

Love Always,

Uncle Paul, God-Dad Paul, Brother Paul, Son, and Child of God.

Walking – the first independent accomplishment one makes as an infant/toddler. Prior to this, we are dependent upon our village for support (feeding, changing, bathing, etc.). For this goal to be achieved several things must occur. First, one must come to a point of being fed up being dependent on others. Having to be carried around is nice, but am I going where I want to go or where others are headed?

This leads to the second realization – vision.

You begin to imagine yourself without barriers. No more being carried around, no more walkers/strollers, no more crawling. You see the destination and with encouragement from your village you stand tall and begin to move on your own. It is rocky at first. You stumble/fall a few times; however, you get up and persevere until vision is completed.

The same occurs in adulthood. As life happens we are sometimes knocked down and may even feel like we're knocked out. In those times we must revert to those primary principles: getting fed up, getting a vision, getting back up and back in place in life. Teaching ourselves to walk again.

When my friend and my brother Paul inquired about a book from God, Learning 2 Walk Again was birthed. I hope this book encourages, motivates, and blesses your spirit deeply to walk to your own rhythm of life.

Peace, Love and JOY!
Willie J. Broussard, Jr.
MBA

CHAPTER ONE

"Life"

The Amazing Thing About Life Is That You Get to Live It

From the first time I was aware of my breathing, what color my skin was, who God was to me, and how everything connected to life, I was extremely disappointed that one day it would all come to an end. I don't know the day, the time, or the hour, but I was ready for it to end before I began to live. I began to plan my exit without realizing or understanding that the middle is where it counts and where the true work is.

The spirit of fear had taken me to the end of life, and I hadn't tapped into my purpose yet. I hadn't tapped into the experience of life, nor did I understand what faith was about and how it, alone, would carry me to the future that was meant for me. I had never considered that my ancestors had prayed for a better life for me without even knowing my name, without knowing my mother's name, and without knowing my grandfather's name and so on. They prayed for my life to be purposed, and they made a great sacrifice for me by doing so. I could not comprehend that I was robbing them of the seed of faith they had planted on my behalf for a life that they wanted but were not able to live.

I now know that I am a part of a cycle of life that goes back as far as my research led me—and then some. What I know for sure is that I am a part of God's DNA. God breathed into me my purpose and the journey that allows me to experience more good than bad. Genesis 2:7 says, "*Then* the Lord God formed the man of dust from the ground and breathed into his nostrils the breath of life, and man became a living creature."

Life for me has not always been a great experience, but it has made me stronger. I grew up without a father, and with a mother who was never consistent with showing me love, with a family who didn't live out loud and own their truth.

Unbeknownst to us, we were continuing a cycle that was given to us by humans and not ordained for us by God. I believe that my family was only living to get through the day and was dwelling in the past, never looking toward the future for a better outcome. Whenever I witnessed my aunts and my mother engaging with each other, there always seemed to be a sense of anger and bitterness that they understood they lived in and that they would not let go. I always had the impression that this made them happy, and it never made sense to me.

As I look back, I think the expectation for a purposeful life was never high enough for them to embrace, so they never lived; they only existed. I truly believe that my mother and her siblings never understood their history, nor did they understand their own purpose that God had for them and that what was for one was not for the other but together they could be a powerful force. I don't think they understood that it was impossible for them to pass the spirit of excellence to me and their other children.

My goal in life, from as far back as I can remember, has always been to find out how the cycle of life began for me and my generation. I first had to embrace who I was and become a lover of life. This would be a challenge that I would never achieve until I understood forgiveness, until I embraced my history, and until I understood who God was to me and His purpose for me and me alone. The next thing for me to understand was that with each setback, fall, bump in the road, knockout, or knockdown that life had afforded me, I had to truly understand that life still goes on, especially when I want it to end.

In life, our goal should be to understand fully that with each setback there is the opportunity to allow God to set us up for the next level in our journey. We can never go to the next level until we fully understand the test. Each test then becomes our testimony to help others overcome their tests. This becomes a pattern that ensures that the next person who walks through his or her problem, situation, or obstacle will be allowed to walk through it with the confidence in knowing that he or she will make it out and be victorious in life.

While we are assisting others in their journey, we must assure them that mistakes will happen and that they will have obstacles in the road every now and then, and that they will fall. But through it all, they will have the ability to get back up and start over to pursue their purposed life that was destined for them to achieve.

There is an old spiritual song that says, "If I can help somebody, then my living shall not be in vain." Service is the key, being selfless is the example, and giving to those who are in need is the blueprint for a life well lived.

To truly understand the meaning of life, you must first understand the cycle of life. When you have embraced the meaning of sharing your experience with others, then and only then will you walk in your truth. As for me, in order for the cycle of life to work effectively, it has always started with God and embracing my ancestors and the seeds that they planted. Now I get to live in the fullness of God while operating in my truth. The process for me to operate in my truth and to get to where I am going has been to relearn, rethink, and redo all that has been taught to me over the years that has never really agreed with my spirit.

What I heard from my elders and what I learned from what I saw and what I embraced from them was ego. Ego has always been the biggest problem in my family. Ego has taught me to do, move, and sometimes speak without thinking, to live without breathing, and to never trust who I was called to be. That was a hard pill for me to swallow.

I soon discovered that this is what I was taught by my mother. I am certain that she had no idea that this was a cycle; that she was continuing this trait from her father, and it was passed to him from his parents and the slave owners who owned them.

I also learned to embrace being absent while being present. This trait I learned from my father, who has never been present in my life. I later learned that his Baptist minister father, Edward Robertson, was never a part of his life, and he passed this trait on to my father.

Both of my parents took on the broken spirit of rejection, and I became the result of two lustful people who saw sex as love. This was the result of their one encounter: my mother's first sexual experience and my father's lust for women. Their need to feel wanted was passed on to me.

I was conceived on September 18, 1967. It was my mother's twenty-first birthday. Both of my parents were still dealing with the spirit of rejection, brokenness, and pain given to them through the cycle of life through their parents until their deaths. I have made it my personal goal to break the cycle.

A lot of what I saw in them that was wrong, I see in me. I have often wanted to fix that part of me that felt unloved and unwanted and needed to be validated. My problem was that I lived in fear and shame. I never allowed myself to move to the next level that was for me. Many times, sex, drugs, and alcohol became my escape from reality, and they were setting me up for failure. My reality became my fantasy, and my fantasy then became a quick fix. This process became toxic for my purposed life.

When you become what you think you are in a drug-induced or intoxicated state of mind, you then believe what you are feeling, and it never ends well for you or the people in your life. Your way of thinking becomes cloudy and becomes your new normal, but it is not normal for your purposed calling in life.

I began to question my life and why I was given my gender, skin color, and family. Life for me was not living my truth, nor could I see my purpose. It became a lie that I lived in black and white with blinders on. I was just existing, with no purpose or desire to live out loud. This soon became my rock-bottom moment, my end of the road, and my I-don't-care way of thinking.

While at the end of the road and while at my rock bottom, I was able to stop, stand still, look up, and ask for help and a better way to be the best me I could be. So I asked God to show me who I truly was, what my purpose was, and what His plans for me were. I had to be open, willing, obedient, and ready to do as He instructed. I had to remove myself from everything that was my normal way of doing things and embrace a new normal that was destined for me to fully operate in.

That meant I had to change the space that I was living in, the people I was involved with, and the city I lived in. I also had to renew my mind. I had to learn to replace lust with love. I had to reexamine every area in my life and everything that was taught to me that did not agree with what was my true purpose. More importantly I had to change my walk with Christ. The path I was on was my mother's path and not my own. I would soon learn that how she viewed God was not how I viewed Him. This changed everything for me.

I had to put away the Me-Myself-and-I way of thinking and embrace the idea of what I could do for others. I was committed to changing everything that was not helping me to walk into my calling. My first lesson was to learn how to walk again, to embrace the path that was set up for me, to lead with my heart and not with my mind, and to teach with that same passion in my heart. My spiritual mother once told me, "Stop thinking with your mind. God wants your heart." That one statement changed my life forever and has been one of my greatest spiritual encouragements of faith.

My journey to this place in life has been rewarding, refreshing, and humbling. Learning to walk again has allowed me to build a better temple and to honor God and my temple with dignity and respect. It has allowed me to acknowledge the purpose that was intended for me and prayed for me by my ancestors. While it has not always been easy and I have certainly stumbled, I've always been able to get back up and keep fighting. I have allowed myself to love me, to forgive me, to embrace the calling that God has planned and purposed for me. It is my duty and honor to share with you the lessons that I have learned on the road into my season and all of the seeds that have been planted in my life that I have embraced along the way. It has allowed me to learn to walk in the divine calling that was ordained for me. This book is my offering to others, to show them how, with God's grace and mercy, you too can walk in God's divine calling for your life.

CHAPTER TWO

"Growing Up"

When you raise up your expectations, you celebrate your ancestors.

I often wonder how my life would have gone if I had been given another name or had been born into a different family. There have been many times I can recall me day-dreaming of having another mother and another life that seemed to be better than the one I had. I didn't grow to love my family until I became a man and was able to see other families interact with one another. I began to realize that, while my family was broken in many areas, our family was not the only family with these issues.

This was the path I had been chosen to walk in and live. With God's help I was able to embrace all the brokenness that came with being born into my family. I later learned that broken people live what they are shown, not what you wish for them to be, especially if they don't see and/or know how to break the chains that bind them in their minds.

I must say that growing up with my family has been a blessing for me. I have had the great fortune to know all of my mother's sisters and brothers and their children. It has allowed me to see that I wasn't the only one who recognized that something about our family was different. There was a brokenness about our parents that could not be put into words. They were only able to express their deeply rooted pain the only way they knew how, in pain.

Growing up in D.C. was an amazing experience for my life that allowed me to enjoy the rich history of the Nation's Capital. It kept me busy and away from home so that I would be out of my mother's view. I was able to escape the pain that I saw and felt from her by staying as active as I could. Many people would say that she was abusive both verbally and physically. I can now look back and say she was only doing what she was taught by her father, who was also taught to express his feelings in his brokenness. Many times she kept her pain bottled up inside, and I was often the outlet that she used to express that pain on. As a child I hated her for it.

My mother's life was filled with shame and embarrassment at the hands of her father who raised all nine of his children -- seven girls and two boys -- with an iron fist. He was the head of his house and he made no apologizes about how he operated in his domain. He spoke to his children and my grandmother, his wife, with authority, and he didn't tolerate back talk or any attitude. If he didn't like how his children talked, walked, dressed or even smiled, he would punish them. As my mother once told me, his words could cut them deeply like a knife. When he would chastise them, he would go on and on for what seemed like hours. When he would discipline them, he would tell them, "I'll beat you until I see blood."

Mother once told me the only time they knew peace in their home was when he was gone. When he was there, they would walk on eggshells and try their best not to move, breathe, or say anything that they thought would upset him. He never expressed love to them in any way such as hugging them, kissing them, or encouraging them. When they achieved recognition in school or church, he said nothing. When guests would come to the home, they were viewed as the help, cleaning, serving and being ready to be put on display. In those days children were seen and not heard.

The children went to one church, while he and my grandmother went to another church. The children ate one thing, while he ate and was served another. Many times he would instruct his children to cook his meals for him. He always made sure that any boy who looked at his daughters or even walked by his home knew that the Eubanks girls were good Christian girls and that boys were not welcome.

My mother once shared a story with me. When she was in her early teens, she was outside with her neighborhood friends, many who lived on the same block. Boys being boys, sometimes showing her that they fancied her was hard. Because she knew the rules, she wouldn't give them any chance in hell.

One particular day while running up and down the street, my grandfather sat in the window watching her. He then called for her to come into the house. When she came indoors, he wanted nothing. He just stood there and looked at her for a few minutes. Then he instructed her to go back outside. He told her to take her Bible and a chair and sit in the front yard and read it until he told her to come into the house. She said she couldn't understand why he would do that to her in front of the whole neighborhood. As she walked outside crying with her chair and Bible, all eyes were on her. She did as he had instructed her to. The other kids laughed and pointed at her calling her names. She said she felt so humiliated. The whole time he just sat and watched her and he said nothing, with a smirk on his face.

Because of this she had a hard time finding love and letting any man into her heart. She never trusted men and she didn't know how to let them treat her like a queen. If she did meet a good man and he said the slightest thing that she did not agree with, it was over just like that. In her eyes if she saw any signs of her father, it was not a chance she was willing to take. Many of the men who wanted to fix what they did wrong walked away not understanding what they did that was so bad that it couldn't be repaired.

If her father was seen as the devil, her mother was seen as an angel. My mother honored her mother until her death. My grandmother did everything for her husband and her children. She cooked, cleaned, made clothes, and even gave my grandfather nine children out of wedlock. My mother said she saw love in her mother's eyes for him and she just could not understand how a woman who was so sweet could love a man so evil.

What they lacked from their father they got from their mother: kisses, hugs, encouragement, and she knew how to talk to them and not at them. Even as a young child I can recall my grandmother being very warm and tender with me, always giving the best hugs and rewarding me with treats, kisses, and love. She was always about her family. She had two sisters who did not play with my grandfather and had no problem voicing their opinion when they saw him going too far.

Grandmother was his second wife and he was her first love. I can see it in photos that I have of them. The love she had for him was evident. In many ways she is a strong presence in my life. I feel her love pushing me daily, speaking into my life, allowing me to feel how proud she is of me and the man I have become. Had it not been for my grandmother telling my mother to get me into Bible school, I would not have the relationship I have with Christ today.

Growing up Eubanks for my mother was the best of both worlds, good and evil. I would imagine this is something my mother never knew how to balance in her life while raising me. Growing up I can count on one hand how many times I heard my mother tell me she loved me. She showed her love by buying me things. But I always felt her pain and her hurt. I never understood where it came from. I not only saw it from her but many times I viewed her as mean, bitter, and angry. When life was rough for her she made sure I knew it.

She never talked to me. She almost always yelled at me. I became a master at tuning her out, and to this day I do not tolerate anyone yelling at me. When she wasn't yelling at me, she was hitting me. She never had a problem with embarrassing me in front of people. If I was on the phone, she would walk by and hang it up while I was talking. If the person I was talking to called back, she made it known that my time with talking to them was over. I can recall many times she made me feel less than human.

One particular incident sticks out in my head that I never forgave her for until I was an adult. I must have been about ten when we were in church one Sunday evening. A lady from the church was giving us a ride home and she asked me to go look for my mother. My mother was also looking for me so we kept missing each other. When I finally found her in the lobby, or she found me, she smacked me so hard I hit the wall. My mouth was bleeding and I was in complete shock.

Another woman who witnessed the whole thing said to her, "He was looking for you." My mother then turned and yelled at her and told her to mind her own business and stay out of hers. Everyone standing around just looked at us. I could see I was the center of attention and it was not a pleasant feeling. The woman put her hands up in the air as if to say, I'm sorry I even said anything. It was the one time I felt like someone stood up for me and saw that my mother was wrong. That would not be the last time something like this would happen to me but it would be the last time I would cry in public.

Because of this event I would learn how to put up a wall and block life out and not allow anyone in. Life as I knew it would allow me to dream of being in another place at any given time and create a world far away from the home I lived in. I would become a problem child in school and act out for attention whenever I could get it. This would only make matters worse for me in our home. Growing up would become my greatest challenge in life. This cycle that passed to my mother from her father and maybe from his mother and the Eubanks family that owned my family would have to be broken. I would first have to get to the root of the problem and break the chains that held us in bondage in our minds.

Growing up Eubanks for my grandfather all began on a plantation in Virginia. His mother Callie Eubanks was born in 1867 on that same plantation owned by George Eubanks in Pedlar Amherst, Virginia, along with her three sisters, Sarah, Marie, Evie, and their father Sammy Eubanks. I would imagine the life of a slave would create pain so unimaginable that I would never be able to comprehend their way of life that was their normal everyday living. I would never understand how they could allow anyone to speak to them as if they were children, being seen as nothing less than cattle and working until they were told to stop. They would live life with no freedom. And for my great grandmother who was raised without the love of her mother, she was then expected to raise up, cook, clean and care for her master's children while her two children were seen as property and she was not able to give her children the attention that a mother wants to give.

She would be forced to watch them work the fields from the time they were able to walk and talk. My grandfather never was given the tools to give to his children the life that every parent wants for their child, simply because he didn't know what that was. At sixteen he went into a segregated Army to fight for a country that didn't see him as a man, who treated him like he was a boy, and who was seen as the help and not a helper. This way of life that he knew and lived, I would imagine, would play a huge part in teaching him how to impart a disruptive way of thinking and living into his children.

Growing up Eubanks and living as a Eubanks must have been for him two very different worlds. One, on a farm living amongst the animals while working the fields and never truly knowing who his mother was or experiencing a normal childhood. While he could read and write, he had to keep it a secret and never let anyone know. The other Eubanks: a working father trying to provide for his children a life that he wasn't sure they would ever achieve, but he knew he wanted a better life for them no matter what. I am sure he wanted his children to live the American dream, even if it meant America didn't think they deserved to dream.

The courage he had to keep pushing to achieve to live his best life while broken is inspiring to me. As for my mother, she had no example as to how to fully embrace love with the confidence that she was operating in an effective love life. Her mother clearly sat quietly while her father imparted his damaged spirit into his children. While I know she loved her mother, I am sure there was a bit of resentment towards her for not standing up to her father and protecting her from his misguided ways. I am sure her confusion played out in her relationship with her siblings, and most certainly, it did with me. In many ways her actions demonstrated to me how not to love, and most of all how to never allow my anger to take control over my emotions.

Growing up in this cycle was hard for me. However, having the perfect balance of love, mercy, and grace certainly gave me the strength to walk my path, to be mindful when I needed guidance, and have the courage to correct my wrongdoings in life. Courage is not defined by what other people may see and/or say to you that you should correct in your life; it is your willingness to stand in your truth and be fearless to challenge yourself to do the necessary work for you to live your best life out loud. It takes boldness to look at your past and not allow it to define your future.

CHAPTER THREE

"Why All The Pain"

*When you celebrate what's wrong in your life, you kill
all the possibilities that are trying to live in you.*

When a child is born into the world there is no reason for him or her to ask why it is that they see and hear what is in their daily life. Their way of doing things becomes the foundation of who their parents want them to be. We quickly learn the golden rule: Do as I say and not as I do and don't ask why. As an adolescent we learn to accept the why and the rules that come with our parents' way of rearing us, because they lay the foundation of establishing who we are and what our purposed life is.

As a teen we begin to view our parents differently. We see their flaws. We see their love. We see their suffering. And we see their joys. Unfortunately, we see their pain as well. When this becomes our reality and our new normal, the questions begin to surface in our minds and we begin to research our hearts trying to figure out just who we truly are. This is never an easy task to obtain. However it does become our ultimate quest in life to either be or not to be like our guardians until we conquer what the truth really is and who they are. Why do we ask why? Because we can.

As a child I always viewed my mom as the most beautiful woman on the planet. We always lived well, not lacking for anything in our home. From the front of the house to the back, every room was immaculately decorated. Our living area looked like a showroom in a furniture store. We had a crushed blue velvet sofa with a matching chair with glass table tops, beautifully decorated drapes from ceiling to floor that matched the furniture. Accessories were perfectly placed throughout the home as if we were ready to be photographed for Better Homes and Gardens. My room and my mom's bedroom were completely furnished with top-of-the-line quality furnishings.

We had all of this, along with closets full of clothing and shoes for every day of the week and then some. To this day I pride myself on my shoe game, always on point and always matching in some way what I am wearing. Whenever we had guests that entered our home, whether it be my adolescent friends or my mother's co-workers, church members, or our family and friends, we were always complimented on how clean and beautifully decorated our home was. It was a great reflection of how we looked to the public on the outside. If only the public could see the mess we carried inside behind closed doors and how we were living.

All the pain that was so deep in our spirits, only a few could see it from time to time, only because a mistake was made and exposed our secret. Most of our neighbors didn't see it, but they heard it as I suffered from the daily pain inflicted on me by my mother. I tried to understand why we had to live in this façade, faking our lives. I often wonder, if God sees all and knows all, surely, He can see how we are living. As a child my mom's looks could sometimes frighten me so much so that at any given moment I could wet myself. I never understood why we couldn't just talk about our problems. She had only one solution to handling any wrongdoings in our home, and that was with pain, hurt, and anger. It was as if it was perfected for her and tailored for us to live this way without veering or requesting a solution that would benefit us both.

As hard as I tried -- and I tried very hard -- to act as if we lived the perfect life, many of my friends would ask, "Why does your mom always look so mean all the time?" I became a master at shrugging my shoulders and quickly changing the subject. The truth of the matter was, I truly didn't know nor did I understand. It was just something I learned to live with. Some days were great; other days were good; many days were just okay. But the ones that stood out to me were always the ones filled with pain. Little did I know that all of the questions that plagued my mind and the pain that I saw in my mother's eyes that I felt from her, the outlet that she used was abuse taken out on me. I would get my answer in the strangest and most shocking way. Sometimes life has a way of showing you things when you least expect it.

It was 1989 and I can recall the phone ringing in the middle of the night. I heard my mother's voice saying to the person on the other end of the call, "What's wrong?" "OK. I'll be there in a minute." She then jumped up running out of the house telling me, "I'll be back." The next morning when she came home she told me my grandfather, her father, had passed. He was 89 years old. She had no emotions. She expressed no sadness. She never cried. It was as if she was relieved. It was as if a weight had been lifted off of her shoulders. For the first time in my life, my mother looked as if she had been liberated. I could see in her eyes that there was peace. This peace would only last for a moment.

After my grandfather's homegoing service the whole family went to my Aunt Edith's house for the repast. My mother's sisters and a few of her nieces and nephews were all in attendance. As I looked at each of my aunts, I could see a familiar look that they each shared. It was as if I was looking at my mother through their eyes. It was the look of pain and relief. As the night unfolded they all, one by one, began to share their memories of their childhood and the lack of love that they had for their father. They each told their heart-wrenching story of abuse, abandonment, neglect, and being unloved. I also could recognize in the faces of my cousins that while the stories that our mothers were sharing about their youth were not our stories, we all could relate to what they were saying. The difference was we never experienced the emotional or physical abuse at the hands of our grandfather; but we certainly experienced it at the hands of all of our mothers.

Not one story that they expressed demonstrated love or compassion from their father, nor did it detail any love that they had for him. This for me was sadder than the service. And it all began to make sense. All those years of me asking and wondering why, all came together that night and my questions were finally answered. This night would open many doors for me and it allowed me to look into the past that they experienced and the reason why I felt the wrath of what was my normal daily life. In that moment I could see in the faces of my cousins that I didn't stand alone.

Many of my cousins began to share their stories with me over the years. They began to express the pain they felt from their mothers that was demonstrated through abuse. My cousin Kenneth shared that at age 14 he was tired of being beat daily by his mother, so he ran away from home and he did not return until he was of the age of 19 years old. And even then he never quite felt like his mother truly loved him. While she may have expressed it verbally, she never showed it with emotions. From the beginning of his life he was left with our grandparents to be reared. He being the first cousin, the first grandchild and the first boy carried the weight for all of us. My grandparents' love for him was very different than the love that they expressed to my mother and her siblings.

So when my aunt came for him at a later age, he really didn't know her or her kind of love. This pattern of pain began to manifest itself in his life and it was a complete culture shock for him. He didn't like it nor did he understand it. My aunt being reared the way she was by my grandfather, she was not capable of verbally expressing to him and demonstrating the love that he was accustomed to, to make him comfortable in his new normal. He had a total shift in his life coming from a two-parent home that validated him when he walked into a room. This culture shock that he experienced when he moved with his biological mother was different. It was not a love that he was familiar with.

The expression of discipline that she exposed him to was certainly taught to her by her parents. I would imagine that my grandparents, in particular my grandfather as he aged, became a more humble, disciplined, soft-spoken person who expressed his love to his first grandchild and his first grandson who, in many regards, was the apple of his eye. While his mother, who he didn't know, had no idea how to embrace him and show him her love. In many regards his life was literally turned completely around and he was thrust into a world that he had no idea even existed.

My grandparents raised him as a young Baptist Christian. His mother had become an American Muslim under the leadership of The Honorable Elijah Muhammad. He had to embrace this new normal and come to grips with his hormones and his sexuality that involved emotions and feelings of being gay growing up in New York City. My cousin Kenneth once expressed to me that his mother in his eyes was not nice to him. She perfected being a hypocrite, living one way in the home and another way outside of the home. This was a pattern and a statement that he made to me that I knew all too well.

When all you see is anger and you have no idea where it comes from, you begin to create your own outlet in life to save yourself and find people who become your family. Kenneth's family became the streets. And for him it turned out great until AIDS took his life. While he certainly had mixed feelings about his mother, he never stopped loving her. His sister said she also saw at an early age that her mother clearly exhibited some issues that she feared she would repeat and it would manifest itself in her children.

I've watched my aunts express this cancer that their father passed to them and how it scarred them as children, teens, young adults, and parents. The problem is I don't think they fully understand what they passed to their children and how it mentally and, for some of us, physically scarred us for life. Many of my cousins have viewed our mothers as mean, angry, bitter, self-centered, confused women. As for me, it has been somewhat different because I have become aware of the cycle and generational curse that is in their blood line. I have forgiven my mother because I am aware of this issue, and she and I have worked on moving past it, but not without doing the work to break the cycle. Before her death I still would encounter her verbal tone and sometimes selfish way of doing things.

Even as an adult many of my cousins and I have experienced the cycle of pain from each other's mothers. Many years ago while living in Dallas, Texas, my mother went into the hospital for what was to be an in-and-out surgery to have a heart valve replaced. I waited for her to return home that night or the next morning to see how things went. When I didn't get a phone call from her, I began to call around to see if I could locate her. To my surprise no one knew where she was and panic kicked in at an all-time high for me. I finally found her in the local hospital and was told that she slipped into a coma and they could not pull her out of it. To make matters worse, they would not give me any information over the phone because they didn't know who I was. I called her sister to tell her what was going on and asked would she be able to check on her and to inform the staff of who I am so that they could release the necessary information to me so that I could see if I needed to come home or not.

My aunt's response to me was cold. I could feel it over the phone. After two days or so I called her back to see if she found out anything, and when she picked up the phone I knew it was not going to be good. She first asked,

"What do you want?" I very calmly asked her what I needed to know. She then said to me in the most chilling way, "I don't know. Why don't you call her church and find out? Stop calling me." Then she hung up on me. I stood in that space in time completely shocked at what I had just heard from her. This was a woman I had known all my life, and she acted as if I was a stranger off the street and she had no time for me. The next day I booked a flight home and handled matters for myself, all to walk into the hospital room to find my mother sitting up in the bed talking. That was the last time I spoke to my aunt in almost ten years. The next time I saw her was at a childhood friend's funeral. She looked right past my mother who was standing there and treated her as if she didn't know her. It was the saddest thing I had ever seen in my life.

Another aunt who lived in New York City found comfort in the streets, and drugs became her way of hiding her pain. Amongst a few of my relatives, we call it The Family Curse. What I know for sure is that pain, when not dealt with, will manifest itself in many different forms as an outlet to release itself from Pandora's box. It will manifest in our physical state, mental state, through drugs, sex, alcohol, depression, and, for many people, suicide, if it isn't dealt with properly. I have dealt with all of these issues trying to figure out Why Me? Depression has been my biggest demon. I have mastered the facade of looking the other way, keeping things bottled up inside, drinking to forget, and doing drugs to feel good. Sex became my weapon of mass destruction because it allowed me to feel wanted even if it meant I was being used. All these things have allowed me to play Russian roulette with my life and not care about the end result.

Psychological pain forced on me by others only meant one thing. Somewhere in my life, more than likely my childhood, a door was opened in the spirit that allowed this way of thinking and living to be normal. My goal was to take me out of my life by killing myself by any means necessary so that I wouldn't win. When you don't know how to operate in the spirit you can allow the darkness to take over your mind, body, and soul and force you into becoming one thing when you want to be another. Most of my life I became great at balancing both worlds: my faith walk, and the darkness. The faith walk was harder because I didn't enjoy being corrected. So when I was told the truth about myself I would block it. The darkness was easy because I was always numb to what my reality was by drinking and doing drugs. The two things together would allow me to do things that I would not normally do and it felt good. Everything about the darkness is done in the dark so this allowed me to be very private while killing myself in a slow death.

I found out that it was easy to find a drinking partner and imposable to reach out for a prayer partner, because praying in the spirit will always expose you to your truth. God will expose you to some things that will force you to stand and face your reality. Darkness, coupled with drinking and drugs, causes you to be still so that the darkness can block your vision. Faith causes you to keep moving so that that darkness can't have the opportunity to cover you, and it allows the light to guide you to your purposed life.

I cannot tell you how many times I have awakened from my sleep to find a man, woman (and sometimes both) in my bed and how I had no idea who they were or what we did or what their names were. Many times I have awakened to find my wallet gone, clothes gone, and the front or back door wide open. I am a believer and I have no doubt in my mind that it was and continues to be God's grace that keeps me alive.

How do you deal with pain when you don't realize you are in pain? For many years I lived in pain because I learned how to cope with it. I ignored all the signs that were a clear indication to me that something was wrong. I don't believe that anything in life just pops up on you. There is always something in your life that will show you your true self. The goal is for you to pay attention to who you are around and what they offer you. Most people are a reflection of you in some way. If you look at the people who are in your life and you see more wrong than good, you should know that they are seeing the same thing in you. Like-minded people attach to the same spirits, and you can't help them until you help yourself first.

The best way to help yourself is to first take control over your mind and how you think of you. As a man thinks in his heart so is he. That brings me to this point: Check your heart for anything that needs to be repaired, and deal with the pain. The worst kind of pain is sometimes and most often passed to you, and it has manifested itself in a different form. In order to see it, you have to dig deep in your heart and deal with some rooted issues that may not have been caused by you but by the people you have been programed to love. This may be the hardest thing to work on because these people may not truly understand the change that is needed for your life. You have to know that what they think of you has nothing to do with who you are.

Unattended generational curses are inherited and may be the worst if not dealt with. My grandfather lived his pain and didn't do anything to change it. In fact, he passed his pain to his children. Many of his children lived with this poison and passed it to their children, and it became a part of our family's DNA. I made a vow to break the cycle, and I made my mother aware of it before her death. She had to first learn to forgive her father for being a broken man and doing what he taught. I had to learn this lesson myself and forgive her for what she was taught and shown. The choice I made was to see it, speak it, and to cast it down and then kill it at the root. Once this deeply rooted pain is exposed, I don't want you to think that it won't come back to test you in life, because it will. Your job is to never allow it to consume you while you are on your journey to wholeness. Your goal in life should always be to walk in your own divine purposed calling by living life one step at a time. When you achieve this in life, then and only then will you be able to deal with the pain that plagues your mind.

CHAPTER FOUR

"Yes Jesus Loves Me"

*The twelve apostles of Christ and I have one
thing in common: Jesus loves us.*

Establishing love outside of your parents, family, friends, and relatives is something that you aspire to achieve based on the love that you learned from those that have expressed that love to you. I would venture to say that whatever your religious beliefs or practices are that you live by are something that were introduced to you in your youth. You never quite understand or are able to fully embrace it until you have your own personal moment that signifies that this is something solid and that it is a stamp of approval as to who and what you are and what it means to you to live in your truth.

The only way you know that your parents, relatives, and friends love you is because of the expression in the gesture of love that you feel, see, and experience. It's a spiritual movement that is unquestionable. You don't have to think about it, and you know it because it feels right. It agrees with your inner spirit man and you get to live it and experience it daily. So without a doubt you understand that you are loved. Because you understand what this love is, you are able to express this kind of love in return to those who love you. With any love that you experience it is received and it is returned in the same manner in which it has been exposed to.

Whether you are Muslim, Catholic, Jew, Gentile, Baptist, or Protestant the one goal is to understand who is in control of your life on a spiritual level. When you tap into it you understand that this is a different kind of love. This love runs deeper than any kind of love you have ever experienced with your loved ones. It becomes a majestic moment that you embrace and you enjoy living with. This love is sometimes always more than a feeling. This love is something that you can't explain. This love is always unconditional. This spiritual love helps you to move with the flow of life and it allows you to live out loud.

When I first understood who Jesus was and the extraordinary things He did for me with His life, how He lived and died for me and millions of people around the world, I knew without a shadow of a doubt that Jesus loved me. I was honored by it. In fact, I was ecstatic. The ultimate goal for me was to tap into His love and live it. Embracing His agape love and returning the gesture to Christ was an honor. For me everything that I was taught and introduced to as a child about Christ became relevant for me in my adult life. Now I know, understand, and fully embrace why Jesus loves me.

All of those things that I felt as a child that I could not quite put into words and express verbally made sense later in life. I would venture to say that even as a teen I knew who Christ was. However, I still was not quite sure of His legacy. As I write this chapter, there is no doubt in my mind that Jesus loves me unconditionally. I clearly understand who Jesus the man and Christ the God is. My introduction to who He is set me free for this very moment in life. I remember it like it was yesterday.

My mother and I would walk past this red brick building every Sunday on our way to the neighborhood laundry facility. It was in this building I would hear a sound that always pulled me to the second floor. This majestic, heavenly tone was flowing out of the windows into the neighborhood. It was unlike anything I had ever heard before in my life. It made me feel something in my gut and it stirred up a spiritual emotion that I was unaware that was even in me. I always wanted to know what was that sound and are we ever going to stop to go in that building and experience what it was. I would often wonder if mother ever felt what I was feeling. The people in this place always seemed to be happy. And while I never saw who they were, nor did I ever get to know them on a personal level, I felt I had a connection with them, and I wanted to be a part of whatever they were doing.

It was during this time in my life my grandmother was very sick, and she was always giving my mother wisdom and words of encouragement. I can see that after every hospital visit that there was a shift in my mother's spirit and that she was embracing everything that her mother was pouring into her. It was as if she knew something that I didn't know. What she knew and understood was that her mother, my grandmother, was in the transition stage of her life. She told my mother, "It's time for you to make sure that Paul gets into a Sunday school class. He needs to learn the Bible. Go find a church and make sure that it is solid in the Word."

My mother loved and respected her mother dearly, and she did just what her mother instructed her to do. The choice she made for a church home was one of the best decisions she ever made. Not just for her or for me but for the both of us as a family. She found us a church family filled with vision, dreams, and a pastor who would help mold us and give us the tools to help us break the cycle that plagued our family for generations, as far back as 1812.

There was something different about this particular Sunday. Instead of us going to the laundry facility, we both put on our best clothes. My mother was always dressed very well from head to toe. She made sure that I was always wearing the latest fashions for my age and that I mimicked the presentation of pride, culture, and class that she wanted the world to see. While my mother always had impeccable taste for our everyday wear and me for school and she for work, I never had a suit with a tie and dress shoes on. This particular day I wore just that. In a word, we looked good. And although I had no idea as to where we were going, I was ready to be seen. We walked the same path as we did to go wash clothes. What we had on was not for washing.

While walking down the street I could feel the music and the spirit in the air coming from the red brick building that sat on the right-hand side on the corner. Most days we walked in the park that's in the middle of the street between two churches, one on the right and one on the left, both sat on corners. I wanted to go to the church that had that majestic sound. I was for certain that my mother wanted to go to the same building and that she was feeling what I was feeling, so as we headed in that direction, I was so surprised when we went to the quiet church that had no music, no feeling within the air, and to tell you the truth, I can't even recall anything about it. I do remember it was very boring. I was not impressed at all. I guess my mother wasn't feeling it either. She had the same look on her face as I did. We left and I was hoping that we would never return to that place again.

The next week the same routine happened. We had on different suits, different clothing, but still looking good. My only thought was, *Please dear God don't let us go back to that same boring place because I could have taken a nap at home.* As we walked the same path going in the same direction as the week prior, we walked down the other side with all the houses. Once more we could hear the music and feel what was happening on the second floor. When we got to the corner, I felt so excited we were going to check out what all of this commotion was all about. So up the stairs we went. It seemed the people were happy to see us. The smiles and the hugs that my mother received as if these people knew her was unbelievable. This one lady in particular, who I later came to know as Ms. Dorothy Myles, was so nice to us. She walked us up three more flights of stairs.

Now I could clearly hear what we were hearing from the streets. As we walked into the main sanctuary, I was so drawn to the music. I could clearly see the guys playing every instrument that you can think of, and they were good. I wanted to jump up and down and run and yell. This amazing feeling came over me. It was nothing like I had ever experienced before. As the woman with white gloves set us down right up front, I could see everything. I could hardly keep my composure. I could tell my mother was experiencing the same emotions I was. When she got up to clap her hands, so did I. We seemed to fit in, almost as if we had been here before. When they would say, "Amen," my mother said it, almost always at the same time. Well, I followed her lead and said it. I remember thinking that I liked this interaction.

This was the day that my mother introduced me to the church family that I would later know as Union Temple Baptist Church. Every week I looked forward to going to see these people who were so nice to us. I wanted whatever it was they were feeling. I also loved the attention from the women. "Oh, look at those eyes." "You are so cute." "Would you like some candy?" This must be heaven, because I remember feeling pretty good about myself. Union Temple was and still is home for me. Everyone knew everyone, and you could feel a genuine love in the air from one another. My mother must have felt the same way because when they asked if anyone wanted to become a part of this family of believers, they should come, Mother stood. I stood. Mother walked up front and I followed her holding her hand as tight as I could. People began to clap as if we were the stars for the moment. One woman asked my mother a few questions and then took the mic and said, "This is Ruth Eubanks and her son Paul. They would like to become members of our family and take the right hand of fellowship." People began to clap harder as if we had made the right decision.

My focus was on the band and the men playing. Tyrone Whitehead on drums, Anthony Brown on bongos, Wesley Boyd on organ, AJ on bass guitar, and Gospel music legend Richard Smallwood in his prime on piano, along with some of the best singers in the world. R&B diva Angela Winbush, Raymond Reeder who later sang with Yolanda Adams, Ruth Moss, and Sully Edwards, just to name a few. I became a part of the cChildren's Choir and my mother was on the Usher Board and later became a part of the Senior Choir that was made up of very young people. I later learned they were called the Senior Choir because they were the oldest choir in the church. The staple in the church music department was the Young Adult Choir who was made up of mostly Howard University Singers and friends. They were known all over the D.C. area and man, oh man, could they sing.

We would practice at noon, and the young adults would practice later in the evening. I would sit in the back of the church and watch their every move and learn all the parts to all the songs. Songs like "I Love the Lord," "I've Got Something," "He's Able" and many more. Gospel legend Richard Smallwood was fresh out of college, along with most of the members. I knew that their gifts would be exposed to the world one day. I could see that Richard had a gift and he was good at it. Most of the songs that were popular at that time we sang. I thought they were all written by Richard, so in my eyes he was a giant. R&B diva Angela Winbush was a singer in the choir, and every time she would sing, she moved the church to another level. In fact, she was my very first crush. As for me, there was one person who stood out from them all. His name was Sully Edwards. He would sing a song Richard later recorded with the Smallwood Singers called "He's Able." Long before Kim Burrell and Karen Clark was Sully. He was a gift that was ahead of his time. He would stand before the church with his eyes closed and step on every note and destroy it. He would then pick it back up and do it again. He was a master at singing, and I studied his every move and every note.

While the music was rich and filed the air in the temple, Pastor Willie Wilson was and is a man of God who always did church outside the box. His principles were from the teachings of Christ. He walked the walk and taught sound word from the word of God with tools that he lived by. Fellowship, Trust, Truth, Love and Commitment, to name a few. We were the first to have a huge painting of Christ in the main sanctuary. I can recall coming to church and there was brown paper covering the wall. Pastor Wilson had found this young black local artist to do the painting. He had created this image of Christ just as it was written in the Bible. People were crying and praising God, singing and dancing in worship. After church we all stood around for what seemed like hours looking at the work of art. If you haven't figured it out by now, the image was of a black Christ.

We would have this yearly event called a 24-hour marathon for Christ. Churches from all over the D.C. area, Maryland, Virginia and up and down the east coast would come preach, sing and offer their gifts to the Lord filling up every hour. It was the most amazing time in my childhood to see and witness. TV crews, radio stations and newspapers would come to report on the event. If you had a gift that you wanted to present before the people of God, you were welcomed. I saw people walk in from the streets and give their life to Christ on the spot. The last hour would always be amazing. People would always come back, and it was standing room only. During those days Richard and the Smallwood Singers were just starting out and they would close out the event. After 24 hours of straight churching sometimes going past the time slot, we would then turn right back around for Sunday morning service.

Many years later we would have a community event called the Chicken and Chitterlings Parade. This event would later become "Una festival." It would become the largest event on the east coast, bringing in acts from all walks of life from Gospel, R&B, Go-Go, Rap, dancers, and poets. There was always something life changing at Union Temple, and my mother made sure I was always right there taking part in the fellowship.

Pastor Wilson is all about community and building people from the inside out. I was about ten years old when Pastor Wilson told the church that we were going to minster to the men and women on the corners in the area who were drug addicts and alcoholics. He wanted us to not talk church to them but talk love to them and invite them into the church for some soup, coffee, tea, and fellowship. It was his goal that we take back our people in the community and introduce them to a better way of living while they lived their best life. I had come home from school that day ready to do whatever it was that I was thinking about. My mother told me to put my things down and go to the church to help out in any way I could. When I got there I followed the lead of the other adults in the church and served the men and women coffee or tea while the adults spoke to the people or, in those days, rapped to them. The smell of some of them was so strong that it almost made me throw up. I kept doing what was needed. That one experience became the root of my life calling to serve those in need. We cleaned up the street that day, and most of those people became members of our church. This opened my eyes to loving people as they are, meeting the needs of the people, and not trying to make my agenda theirs. It showed me how to love people on another level. Because of that one day, I have never turned my back on those in need. I was a witness to a miracle that day. I saw men and women transform from what the world viewed as nothing to becoming solid people in their life with their families. They took their place in life as Kings and Queens. It was one of my most treasured memories in my life.

The Cobra Drill Team with Brother Ricardo Pain was at that time something I hated, but now looking back, it was so important to who I am today. Brother Ricardo Pain was in the armed services and he formed the drill team with all the youth in the church. He was tough, strict, disciplined, focused, and dedicated to loving us like we were his own children. He was truly a father figure to many of us, and he embraced us in good times and bad. He had no problem calling you out when you were, as he put it, "out of order." We would meet on Saturdays and march in the hot sun, snow, or rain for hours. We went on camping trips. The idea was that they kept us busy and off the streets.

One year we were away on a camping trip and it was my birthday weekend. While lying in the tent in the hot sun, in the woods doing whatever, I was so tired and all I wanted to do was sleep. No one said anything about my birthday and I was over the whole thing. Just as I was about to fall off to sleep, Brother Ricardo called me with this loud voice. "Paul, front and center." When I stepped out, he and the other men were yelling at me to drop down and give them ten. The whole time I was thinking, *Are you kidding me*? All I wanted to do was sleep. So I dropped down, and there was a cake with candles. He then said, "Happy Birthday, son!" All I could do is cry tears of joy and think, *They remembered*. It was a great ending to a long, hot day.

Every year we marched in parades that had a purpose. Our very first event and parade was the MLK parade to fight to get Dr. King's birthday to become a national holiday. All I can recall about that day was that I was cold and I hated it. Later that week my teacher called me in front of the class to salute me for being a part of an important event in the D.C. area. She had seen me on the news and wanted me to share with my class what we did. I had become somewhat of a local celebrity in my school. I will always remember the drill team and the bond we had with one another then and still to this day. 14th and U Street Southeast Washington D.C. We call it now the old red brick building. It will always be home for me in many ways. Many seed moments were planted in my life during that season of growing up. I was not only introduced to Christ. I was also taught that He was not just my mother's God; He was my God also. What I learned from those days was great, and it has allowed me to be who I am and embrace my purposed life.

CHAPTER FIVE

"Toxic Waste"

The Violator can take away your virginity
but he can't take away your identity.

One of the most difficult things in life to deal with is pain that has been exposed, especially pain that has been manifested from your past due to other people's spirits that you have no control over. Pain from your past that you have never spoken about to anyone. Pain from your past that you have buried and have forgotten about because of shame and fear. The worst kind of pain normally is something that has kept you in bondage from living your true purpose in life. Being sexually violated as a child teaches you to live in a shell and to hide your pain deep inside of you and to never talk about it. It also teaches you to never think about it and never acknowledge it. If you are not careful, it can becomes a manifestation of alcohol, drugs, and sexual abuse on others.

I can recall every time someone sexually violated me and the shame that I felt when it happened. At times that shame is still a part of my daily life. I had to deal with that shame almost 40 years later and pray that it never happens to another child as it happened to me. Many times the guilt that I carried from the oppressor weighed my mind down into a deep depression. I often wonder, why me? What was it about me that a grown man and sometimes women would use my virgin body as a sexual tool for their own sexual pleasures? For most of my adult life I often felt the reason why I never truly embraced love was because I didn't understand the difference between lust and the sexual pleasures that go with it and love from the heart.

When I did find love it almost always ended with pain. Pain that caused me to go into depression and pain that never allowed the person who was trying to pursue my love to understand why I was so incapable of loving them back, locking them out by guarding my heart, my emotions, and exposing them to all of my fears. Many times the innocence of my childhood caused me to be vulnerable and accept validation from my oppressor through their form of love and sexual abuse. So when the violations happened to me, I never saw it coming. I thought that this was their way of loving me that I needed to learn from and live with. If misery loves company, it always had a home within my life.

Many years later while in church, the spirit of Prophecy fell on my Pastor Chris Dexter. It allowed him to open Pandora's Box that housed all my secrets. It unleashed my hidden shame that caused me to live in deep depression for so many years. I now know and understand God opened that door for a reason. Ever since that day, I have never been able to close that door, and I have been forced to deal with the sexual abuse that drove me into a world of lust for drugs and alcohol. What I was able to do later in life is to forgive the persons who violated me.

First, I had to journey down a path that has been the hardest thing to think about, talk about, and share with others. This journey has not been easy but it has been necessary because the person who I had to deal with and help first was me. In order to do that, that meant that I had to come face-to-face with my younger self. I had to ask him what was going through his mind and, if I could change anything, what would it have been? What I learned from my younger self is that I just simply did not know. Although I didn't know what I could have done to avoid it, I still can remember every detail and every moment that happened that led up to the abuse.

It was early one morning when my life made a sudden and drastic change that would shape me forever. My mother had a blue suitcase with flowers on it in her hand as we walked out of our one-bedroom apartment in Washington, D.C. We got on the local Metro Bus system. In those days bus fare was $0.40. I clearly remember her giving me the money so that I could put my own coins into the box. I had no idea where we were going but I do recall there was a drunk man who was very fresh with every woman on the bus. He made me very uncomfortable. He used foul language and he smelled like a brewery. He, for some reason, kept talking very disrespectfully to my mother. He even got on the floor of the bus and looked up her dress and told everyone what color her underwear was. This was one of those moments in my life that I can clearly recall feeling angry.

But my expressions showed fear because I was very afraid of what he might do to her. In my young child-like mind, I kept wondering why the bus driver would not stop the bus and say anything to him or tell him to get off the bus. This would be my first introduction to pain by a man that I didn't know, but it would not be my last. As the bus came to a stop we stood up and walked off. Then came the walk into an unknown area in southeast D.C. We walked down this long driveway. At the end of the driveway was a very ghetto-looking building. It almost looked abandoned. Up the stairs into this hallway, then down the stairs into the darkness. My mother seemed to know where she was going so I trusted her. But I would not let go of her hand. She then knocked on the door facing us. When the door opened, a woman with a bright smile opened the door. She seemed to know my mother by her name. "Hello, Ruth. How are you?" My mother replied, "I'm well. Thank you." "This must be your son Paul. Look at those big pretty eyes."

How did she know me and how did she know my name, was the question that came to my head. My mother said to me, "Say Hello." She took my mother's suitcase and they sat down for what seemed to be small talk. All the while, while they were talking, I kept wondering to myself, *Why are we here?* And I had to go to the bathroom really bad. I must have been holding it the entire ride on the bus. I assumed that the woman must have sensed it. She looked at me and said, "Do you have to go to the bathroom?" I replied, "Yes." She took my hand and took me to what seemed like the smallest bathroom in the world. It was my first time ever seeing a half bath. When I was done I felt so relieved but anxious to get back to where my mother was. When I walked out of the bathroom, my mother was gone. It was my first time but it would not be my last time feeling like my mother had abandoned me.

The woman who I will call Ms. C took my hand and escorted me around this unknown place. It was a huge apartment with three bedrooms, a dining area, living room, and two bathrooms. It was well decorated and it smelled like someone was cooking bacon. It was extremely quiet. It was quiet because it was still very early in the morning. Ms. C told me to take off my clothes and get into the bed in the back room that we had walked into. She told whoever was in the bed to move over. The covers moved and a head looked up at me. "Hey, man." I said hello and I got into the bed. I can recall the bed being very warm and the person in the bed smelled like soap. All I could think of was, *Why would my mother bringing me here? Why didn't she say goodbye to me? Why didn't she tell me where we were going? Did she give me away to this family?* As the tears rolled down my face, off to sleep I went.

I kept thinking to myself whoever this person was must have known I was afraid. They pulled me close to their warm body. They were holding me like they knew me but something kept poking my back. When I reached behind me to see what it was, they took my hand and placed it around what seemed to be a flashlight. Now my eyes are open but I can't see. My hand was covered with their hand. Then they said to me, "Keep rubbing it." *Keep rubbing what?* Was the first thought in my head. *Who are you and what is it that I am rubbing that seems to be warm? Why are you making noise in my ear?* I had no clue as to what was going on. This would be my first sexual violation. Then all of a sudden it stopped and the lights came on and I heard the familiar voice of the woman.

"Y'all get up." From the top bed then jumped down this tall, lean brown body and then another one. The voice behind me said very clear and calmly, "I'm up, Ms. C," then walked out of the room. "Damn, she almost saw it," he said under his breath. I could now see that there were other people in the room with us. Someone said to the other, "Is this Paul?" The other person responded, "Yep, this is him." They must have known what happened because they smiled at each other as if they had planned it. In my head I was still thinking to myself, *Why was there a flashlight in bed with us?* When I stood up after getting out of the bed. I reached behind my back to wipe off what I thought was sweat, and on my hand was an extremely large amount of white cream. I said out loud, "What is this?" The person in the bed with me immediately got a towel and wiped me off.

When I came out of the room, there was Ms. C, standing there topless. I was in shock. I could not stop looking at her. I couldn't believe what was going on. There were so many people in this room, and why is she standing here topless? It was my first time ever in my life seeing a woman in that manner. I was their guest for the summer and this would become my introduction to a long summer that would force me to walk into Pandora's Box and never look back. I had so many unanswered questions in my head. After a while those questions became my reality. I got accustomed night after night to her sons taking turns laying me on my stomach while they rub their genitals on me until they ejaculated. Then they would clean me up and go to sleep.

One particular day we were laying in the bed. I was laying one way while the other person was laying another. The next thing I knew, my hand was being pulled. Because I was now aware of the routine, I turned on my stomach. This time I was told, no. I sighed with relief and turned on my side. And then he put his penis to my face. "Open your mouth," he said. I shook my head no. I felt fingers in my mouth and then it happened. I could not breathe almost to the point that I was choking but he kept going faster and faster. His legs got stiff, and while his hands were holding my head, he then released himself. I now knew where the white cream came from. He must have told his brothers, because this became a daily thing for me. My hell on earth.

One day I was told that another relative was going to keep an eye on me all day. I thought he was nice to me. We went to the park in his car. We had even gone to McDonald's after picking up his girlfriend who was extremely nice. I felt safe for the first time being in this environment. We later dropped off his girlfriend at her home and proceeded to go back to the empty apartment of Ms. C. He said to me, "Go take a bath. You need to get washed up. I'll run your bath water." So far this was the best day since being here at this house. No one was touching me or intruding on my body. As I pulled down my underwear, he walked into the bedroom naked. In my child-like mind, I thought, *We must be taking a bath together.* He then pushed me on the bed very aggressively. Then I thought to myself, *Not you, too! You have a girlfriend!*

He then began to oil me down. Because I was used to this routine by the others, I just laid there in disbelief that he was now doing what they were doing. But what he was doing was very different from the others. I felt this sharp pain in my butt. Just as I opened my mouth to yell, his hands covered my mouth. I began to fight. I began to cry. I began to yell, but no one could hear me. He was much bigger than I, so my fighting was in vain. His penis was now in me. It was the most excruciating pain I have ever felt in my life. I kept thinking, *Please just let somebody walk in. Please let my mother knock on the door and save me. Please somebody help me and make him stop.* I could not believe that he seemed to be enjoying this as he moaned. He began to sweat all over my body. I began to zone out. That was the moment in my life where I had a major shift and experienced what it felt like to be present in the flesh but to be absent in the mind.

Then the door opened. It was one of Ms. C's sons. He smiled and then closed the door. It seemed like it would never stop. It seemed like it went on for hours, in my mind. This must be what hell feels like. Hot, fiery, burning, and all I can do is cry for help inside. Because of the routine of the others, I knew that the end result would be the white cream, so I laid there and waited. I just didn't know when he would be finished, and so I had to wait for what felt like an eternity. What seemed like hours to me finally came to a screeching halt when he let out a loud sound and his entire body became stiff and he grabbed me and moaned until he was done. Then he laid there on top of me and gave me a kiss on my cheek as if it was a sign of marking his territory. When he was done, reality came back to me. I can now hear and see clearly.

During this whole process I didn't even realize I was crying. He stood up, looked at me, and told me to stop crying like a little bitch, because if I didn't stop crying, I would get in trouble. He then told me that if I told anyone, he would kill me or do the same thing he did to me to my mother. I walked out of the room in shock. I felt what seemed like sweat was running down my legs. I assumed it was sweat but I was expecting the white cream. I reached back to wipe it off, and when I looked at my hand it was blood. He told me to get into the tub of hot water. It burned because he put rubbing alcohol in the water. I felt different. A part of me was taken and gone forever. My first sexual violation came from an unknown set of people that in my child-like mind, my mom had set me up for this to happen. I thought this for many years that she simply did not care for me, because if she did, she would have never allowed this to happen to me. I felt like I was no longer myself and I would not be myself from that moment on for the rest of my life. I was seven years old, and I would have to live with this secret for most of my life.

2535 Jasper Street Southeast Washington, D.C. was a great move for mother and me. She was making great money, so we moved into a bigger apartment with two bedrooms and plenty of space. I had my own room and all the freedom that goes with having a working mom. It was during this time of my life that I was known as a latch-key kid. Mother got up before I did for work so that meant that I was always alone. She would call me to make sure I was up and ready for school after I had breakfast and dressed to start my day. The rules were very simple: Make sure I did my homework after school and make sure that there was no one in the house. I was not allowed to go outside unless I called her to ask. My room had to be clean and I was to stay out of her room and her things.

While I never forgot any of these rules, most of the time I never followed them either. In my mind, this was my house. She just paid the bills and made sure I had food to eat. The joy of being an only child is that I pretty much had what I wanted and my friends saw my house as the place to be. I had my own room, TV, my choice of cereal, new shoes for school and after school, and a closet full of clothing to wear. I had too much time on my hands and no one to watch over my movement every day.

One day I decided I was not going to go to school and that I would enjoy myself in her bed and watch her TV. That got old for me real fast. So I went outside to sit on the front porch and read an Ebony magazine. The next building over from our building was a man who I had seen many times before. I also knew his two stepsons who were around my age. He was well-known in the neighborhood so he was no stranger to me. He came over to speak and asked what I was doing home from school that day. I told him some lie about not feeling well and that my mom knew and told me to stay home and rest. He told me he hoped I felt better and that while I was outside, he wanted to show me something in his building and would I come to see it. We both walked around the back to his building into this empty apartment that was abandoned. All I can recall is the two of us standing in there and him saying to me, "This is a nice place and it's cool in here. It's also a nice place to play with yourself." When he turned around, he had his penis out masturbating himself. The only thing I kept thinking was, *Please don't ask me to put it in my mouth or in my rectum.* While he didn't ask me to do those things, he did ask me to touch his penis and help him masturbate. I could tell he was enjoying my hands on him because he began to moan and he released himself all over the floor.

Just like before, he told me those words that every predator says, "Don't tell anyone or you'll get in trouble." This time I told, but the backlash from the other kids in my area and school was worse than me not saying anything, not only for me but for his wife and their children. The experience of all this would damage me and cause me to suffer from depression that would sometimes turn into anger and rage. I was a ticking time bomb that lacked courage. I feared being alone and I completely hated my life. In a matter of days everything about me had turned from being a great student to being the worst child in my class. The truth for me is that, while I have been a victim of unwanted lust, seduction, and sex from my predators, I, too, would cross the line and come close to being the very thing that I hated about them.

My mother and I lived on the second floor of a two-story unit in another part of Southeast D.C. The first floor was mostly old couples who had lived in the building for many years. They were the eyes and ears of the building, and unlike our other apartment before, they saw and told everything. On the second floor there was our apartment that faced the front of the Main Street Pitts place where we lived. This would be the beginning of my life spiraling out of control. In the other units on our floor were two mothers who also had boys. One of the boys was two years younger than me; another, four years younger than I. Naturally my mother and the other women became close friends because they had so much in common, being single black women raising their children who were boys. I became somewhat of a big brother to them, although I never wanted to. I was fine being an only child and did not embrace the change. Needless to say, we were a tight unit on that floor. So much so that on any given day one or both of the boys was at our place or I was at theirs. Looking back I have no idea why the boys and I were even seen as peers. I was much older than they were.

During this time my hormones were all over the place. I was experiencing wet dreams and my acne was terrible. I had no idea what was taking place in my body. I was never quite able to figure out what to do with my unwanted erections. In fact, I was embarrassed and ashamed of what was going on with me. I had no one to ask questions or talk to about this problem. One day I was wrestling with one of the boys, and without thinking, I got an erection. I didn't notice it but he noticed it immediately, and without thinking, I kept playing with him. When I got up from the floor, he said to me, "Your pee-pee is hard. Can I see it?" I pulled it out and he grabbed it. When he did, I pulled away and yelled at him. I could tell his feelings were hurt. I knew the damage was done and there was no turning back from this craziness that had taken place. I crossed the line and I knew it. So I ran to the bathroom to fix myself. I was completely at fault and wanted it to be over and for him to be gone. I knew no matter how I tried to explain this, I would not come out looking like the good guy in this situation.

When I came out of the bathroom I could clearly see he was sad and that I had hurt his feelings. He wanted to go home to his mother. What I was not going to do was tell him what I was told: that it was his fault and that he would get into trouble. I took him home with the hopes that he would not say anything and that he would forget about it. When his mom opened the door, the first thing he said to her was, "He showed me his pee-pee and got mad at me." The look she gave me said it all. I could see she wanted to kill me. She looked shocked, then I saw rage, then death in her eyes. I tried to change the topic but it was way too late, and I could feel my heart sinking into my shoes.

My mom worked late and got up early. So that night I could not sleep and I waited for her to see if she would be told what happened. The next morning when she got up I was up also. As she walked out of the door, I watched her through the peephole. Our neighbor's door opened and in walked my mother. When she walked out, she walked down the stairs and I could see her on the street with the look of pain on her face. There was no doubt in my mind that I caused that pain for her. She had no idea how to fix this. That evening when I got home from school, I opened the door to our place, and my mother, our neighbor, and maybe six or seven men from our church along with our Pastor was sitting in our living room. There was no way out of this and I wasn't sure what would happen to me but I knew it was not going to be good.

To this day I could not tell you what they talked about or said to me. I do know that I was in fear for my life. I was for certain I was getting out of this with a slap on the hand or a spanking. Then in slow motion they all got up, one by one, and so did I. Someone handed me my coat and we walked outside to the cars lined up in front of our place. As we drove up the hill on Martin Luther King Avenue, we pulled into the gates of St. Elizabeth Hospital in D.C. It was one of the largest mental hospitals on the east coast. I began to cry uncontrollably but this did not faze any of the men nor my mother who never looked at me the whole time. I kept trying to tell her I was sorry and that I would never do it again. Then my sadness turned to anger at her for letting them do this to me. When it came time for me to go onto the unit I began to fight for my mother's hand, but the men blocked me from touching her. I could see she was in tears also but she never looked at me. She just walked away with them and never looked back at me to say goodbye.

I was taken to one of the units on the floors and all I could remember thinking was that some crazy person is going to kill me and my mother didn't care. This would be another pivotal time in my life where I felt abandoned by my mother. My first day on the floor I was in complete fear. I felt like I was being punished for what I was taught, and this was not fair because I never did to him what was done to me. All the pain I was feeling from my sexual predators was spilling out and I couldn't trust anyone. This was when I made my first attempt to kill myself and end it all. When that didn't work, my pain turned into hate and rage at another level. I became so confused about life and how I was being treated. When one of the staff persons came at me to take off my clothing, I spit at them and yelled at the top of my lungs, "GET THE FUCK AWAY FROM ME!" The next thing I knew, it seemed like hundreds of men came rushing at me, tackled me, took off my clothing, and put me in this room with no bed, just a mat, and locked the doors. I was there for two days, and for most of the time in the room, I cried myself to sleep.

While I was there I learned quick how to play crazy to get what I wanted, and all I wanted was drugs to numb my pain. I went to group meetings and had a lot of one-on-one time with the doctors. Most of the time, I stayed to myself and read books. It was during this time that I began to plan my life to get as far away from D.C., church, and my mother as I could. I hated them all and wanted nothing to do with any of them. My trust was at an all-time low for anyone I knew. I did what I was told. I did not speak to anyone unless I had to, and even then, I said very few words. After a few months I was moved to another unit where the kids there had a bit more freedom. This unit meant the next step was home and I was happy about this move. I was still in deep pain but I knew I could not say anything because if I did they would keep me, and I was not going to let that happen.

These kids were older but nothing like the crazy people on the floor I was on. I later learned that most of the people on the unit were from the court system who came from jail by playing crazy to escape hard time. In their minds, this was heaven. In my mind, this was hell with more freedom. I shared a room with two other guys, one who chain smoked, the other talked to himself. But they both were cool. We played cards, played records, and watched TV. I read almost every book I could get my hands on. The view on this floor overlooking the city was amazing, so I spent most of my time on the closed-in patio looking over the city. I spent my 13th birthday in the hospital, and the staff gave me cake and ice cream. While I looked happy on the outside, on the inside I was not. To me this was a sad way to spend your birthday.

One day while walking the grounds of the hospital, one of the girls told me we had a new guy who was on the floor. She only spoke of him because she thought he was, in her words, the most handsome person she had seen in her life, but she didn't think he liked girls. She called him shady. She said he came to the unit with chains on, so we knew he came from jail. I wanted to rush back to put up my things so he wouldn't steal them. When I got to the unit I can't recall what I was doing. I do remember meeting him and she was correct. He was gorgeous. I could not move or talk. He saw me, and he began to work me from that day. He was very charming, and he had a way of making you feel like you and he were the only two people in a room filled with hundreds.

We quickly became friends, and like me, he didn't talk much, but when he did, even the staff stopped to give him their full attention. Most times he made me very nervous. My spirit told me to follow my gut and stay away from him but I couldn't. One day while in the shower with the others guys, we were talking and laughing, and in walks Roger. As he took off his towel, I got so nervous, I dropped my soap. Like a pro he said without missing a beat, "OH NO, YOU DROPPED THE SOAP!" We all laughed, and he walked over looking at me directly in my eyes and picked up the soap. He stood so close to me I could feel the heat coming from his body. He then handed me the soap and winked at me and said, "I got you, boo." I was being seduced and didn't even know it. I also had a full-blown erection and everyone saw it, especially him. He looked down at it, touching it gently, and told me to put that up. I was so embarrassed.

One night while in bed, he came over and got in my bed to, as he put it, talk. Oddly enough, that is exactly what we did all night, talk. He had a way of making me feel safe. We talked about life and our dreams for what seemed like hours. When he got up to get back in his bed, he kissed me gently on the lips. He did this every night for almost two months. I was so confused by his actions and how he made me feel. I liked it and I didn't want to. I didn't want to feel this way about another guy, nor did I want to be gay. I knew God would not like this, and my mother would not approve.

One night he didn't get in my bed, and I asked him what was wrong. He told me he felt I didn't like him. He was now playing mind games with me and it was working. I said to him that wasn't true. He said if it wasn't true then I should get in his bed. So I did. When I did, I couldn't tell he was naked at first. Then he pushed his body next to me and we talked like we always did. When I went to sleep, I woke up with his hands around my mouth, and he was in me. All I could do was lay there. When he was done, he literally pushed me out of his bed and never spoke to me my entire time I was on the unit. He had planned it and I never saw it coming. The next day one of the counselors called me into the office. One of the boys saw me in his bed and told it. When they asked Roger about it, he said I got in his bed and made him have sex with me and he did not feel comfortable sharing a room with me. They moved me to a single room where I stayed for the rest of my stay on the unit.

The next chapter of my life became unreal for me. I soon learned not to trust anyone, and I also learned to cover up my pain from myself and anyone who tried to get close to me. I would turn my pain into drinking, drugs, and sex. I was so broken that it would take years before I would recover from what happened to me. When you become prey for a predator, your body becomes a playground for their spirit to lay dormant. Most men don't say anything about their rape because of shame of what people will think about them. They feel it will make them look like less than a man. Most people who they tell have a way of making them feel like they are less than a man. When you don't speak about it, it becomes an untreated cancer that eats away at your soul. Many times when it happens, it's a mind game that is being played on you. Talking about it is the first step to curing this cancer. I had to learn that I had nothing to do with the spirit of the persons who violated me. Most often the perpetrator was a victim themselves and they used me to release their cancer.

In order to break the cycle from continuing and you becoming the perpetrator, you have to stand in your truth and recognize that you are not what has happened to you. This means you must change the way you think about yourself and turn all that energy around to be released into the universe so that it can evaporate into the air, never to return. When you speak about what has happened to you, you empower someone else to tell their story, and it becomes a visible sign for others to see clearly what is in front of them. Being a man has nothing to do with you sexually. It means being able to dare to be different even when you are being tested. Most often, women respect other women who speak their truth boldly. I feel this is an area men can grow from and learn from women. When you tap into your inner feelings and allow it to liberate your inner strength, this becomes the best way to regurgitate all that toxic energy that has nothing to do with who you are called to be. This then allows you to live your purposed life out loud with the strength in knowing that you are not who others say you are. When this happens, then and only then will you begin to live your best life with power, love, and a sound mind.

CHAPTER SIX

"Fighting To Survive"

Each time we face our fears, we gain strength,
courage, and confidence in the doing.

I think it's safe to say that my journey into my teen years was hell on earth that I embraced with love and a bit of confusion. I stepped into my manhood and I had no clue as to what I was doing. I didn't want to hear anything that was being told to me. My hormones were guiding me, and as crazy as it may seem to say, I enjoyed sex, drugs, and alcohol, sometimes all at the same time. It was my goal to do it as much as I could, as often as I could, with anyone who would do it with me. My relationship with my mother was all but present. I had no problem with defying any and everything she would say to me. I hated her and being around her. I am sure she felt the same way about me. I was fighting a champ that was good at demonstrating hate. I enjoyed allowing the spirit of pride and my ego to go against what I knew was wrong. I was older and not willing to take her verbal and physical abuse any more than she was more than willing and loved to impose on me.

I think she was aware and hated that it didn't affect me anymore. So she would make it her goal to say whatever it took to cut me deep. Sometimes it worked, but I would never let her see it in my face and I knew it pissed her off. When I saw it got to her, I would smirk and make sure she saw me enjoying defeating her. There were many times we would go days without speaking to each other and that was fine with me. I had become friends with a guy in school name Eric Fleming who also lived across the street from me. Like myself he was an outcast in school. Most of our peers, mainly boys, would kick our asses and chase us home from school.

We hit it off great. The only difference was that he liked his mother and she loved him. But boys being boys, he fought her every chance he could. He ran away from home to prove his point. He left home to stay with a woman name "Juicey." I soon followed him. I can recall throwing my things from the second floor window. Eric stood downstairs under my window to catch my things. I was in such a hurry to get out of my mom's place, I was getting ready to jump. Eric stopped me by yelling at me, calling me crazy. We laughed so hard I didn't hear my mother come in the door. She looked at me and didn't say anything and went into her room and closed the door. I closed my room door and walked out the front door and never looked back. I was such an ass to her and her feelings and I didn't care.

Juicey had two little boys of her own and housed many runaway boys. She was what the young people today would call a Thot. She also had what they called sugar daddies who paid her bills. She would let us have sex with her. I loved having sex with her, and any time I would get an erection I would find her and take it and she loved it. I would follow her in the shower, in the kitchen like a horny goat. She would be sleeping and I would get in bed with her and have my way. She never said no. She even showed me a few tricks. When she was done with me, she moved on to the next guy and would stop me from taking it.

Eric and I did everything together in school and on the streets. When his mother had had enough of him being gone from her home, she came and got him. He told her, "I will only come home if Paul can come. If not, then I won't come." He was truly my brother. What he said do, I did. And whatever I told him to do, he did. We had orgies, smoking pot, drinking and we never went to school. If we did go to school it would be on Fridays to catch up on what we missed. His mother was a drunk who had a boyfriend who didn't like us. We would hear them in the room having sex and pick the lock and walk in on them. He would walk by us and we would stretch out our feet out to trip him up. We would go in his wallet and take all his money, his weed, and his booze. Because of us he never came over, and Eric's mother would stay at his house to keep him happy and to stop us from hurting him. We were such jerks to him.

While his mom was gone we would have parties and lock her out of her own home. The way we did her, I would never be able to get away with that with my mother. One, she would fight back and probably kill us both. Two, I had more respect for her than to do that. This must have gone on for about six or seven months before it would all end. Then one day Eric's mother sat us down and told us something had to give. She could not afford keeping me in her home any more. She wanted to go talk to my mother about where I was and see if I could go back home. We walked to my mom's and knocked on the door. When my mom opened the door she was stone cold in the face and never said one word to me. She only spoke when she was asked a question. She made it clear she did not want me back in her home. She even told his mother I was now her problem and that she saw me one day and went the other way. I must say I was so hurt by her statement I could not believe what I was hearing. When we got up to leave, I was the last one to walk out the door. When I turned to say goodbye, my mother closed the door in my face.

While I was happy to be with my best friend, I was hopeful my mother would fight for me. I was hoping she would beg me to come home and be happy to see me. I kept waiting for her to say she loved me but that would never happen. Another month must have gone by. By this time, I was homesick and depression had begun to creep back into my life. Eric and I had come home from school one day, talking about what we were going to eat when we got home. There was a surprise waiting for us. When we walked in the door there was a woman sitting there with his mother. She was a social worker with the D.C. government. I looked at Eric and we both hugged each other and broke down and cried. In that moment I went into survival mode and began to fight for my life. I told the lady to call my mother; she would not let this happen to me. I could see on the woman's face before she said anything that I wasn't going home. She said she had already spoken to my mother and that I was going with her to a group home. Just like that, my life changed.

I was going to my new normal to a home in uptown D.C., to an area I had never been to and had no idea even existed. It was a beautiful home with four levels to it. The top level was where the bedrooms were and a bathroom. The second floor was where the family who watched me lived. The main floor was the living area, dining area, and the kitchen. The basement had a pool table, TV, and laundry area. It was a home with two live-in parents and their child. It was set up to give children like me a family setting so that we could have a strong unit in place that we could call home.

I stayed in school during this time. I felt like I was a part of a family and I had a sense of belonging with people that wanted me. We had dinner with each other and we talked about our day. It was all good until I learned about smoking pot from one of the other boys in the home. Around the corner from the group home was a store that sold beer to anyone no matter how old you were, as long as you had money. So we were always in the store buying something to drink. If I was a rock star, this life was a perfect fit for me because it was nothing but sex, drugs, and hip hop.

With anything you do, all things must come to an end. And that was the case for me. My mother's family in New York got word I was in a group home, so they sent for me to come and stay with them for the summer. Off to New York City I went. But before I went, my social worker told me my mother wanted to talk to me. I was glad to hear this news. I went to see her at my old apartment. When I got there, she still seemed to be cold to me but she was talking to me. Although she never gave me eye contact the whole time I was there, she told me she was in a relationship with a man and he wanted to meet me. I felt happy for her and I was glad she spoke of me to him. His address was written on a piece of paper on the table. I picked it up and walked out the door to go meet this Mac person she spoke of.

The next day I went to see him not far from where I lived in the 14th Street area of northeast D.C. As I walked up the stairs and rang the bell, I could see into the window. At first I wasn't sure if I was at the correct place because there was a little girl looking at me on the other side of the window. My mother came to the door to let me into the home. As I walked into the home I could not believe my eyes and what I was seeing. There was a little girl, but behind her was three boys in wheelchairs. I looked at my mother as if she had lost her mind. She never looked at me but she seemed to have a great rapport with these kids. Then this short man who was very loud and smelled like cigarettes and alcohol walked into the room. He kept saying my name as if he knew me, with this fake smile on his face. I could not understand what was going on. He then told me each kid's name one by one, Crystal, Easter (named after him), Lester, and Sylvester. They all reached for my hand to shake it. They each asked me was I Ruth's son? I felt like I was tripping.

He then asked me to come downstairs to his office so that we could talk to one another. As I walked through the home, I was still in disbelief as to what I was witnessing. What was my mother thinking? Had she lost her mind? This could not be her new normal that made her happy. Was this better than life with me? My next thought was, I needed a drink. As I go into his office and sit down, he began to tell me about his life. Everything from being a teacher, his first and second wife, the affair he had that brought his youngest daughter into the world. He seemed to brag about it as if I really cared. As a matter of fact, I found him to be very arrogant. He then starts telling me how good of a woman my mother was.

As he is telling me this, he is getting up from his desk. He walks to me and stands in my face and begins yelling at me, "WHAT THE FUCK IS WRONG WITH YOU? WHY ARE GIVING YOUR MOTHER A HARD TIME? YOU UNGRATEFUL PIECE OF SHIT." Then he says to me in a very calm voice, "Get your act together." He then walks back to his desk and sits down very calmly and says, "Now, do you have anything you want to ask me?" I had nothing to say. I just wanted to get the hell out of this place and go. I said to him, "No. I just want to go." Then I stood up and walked to the door nearest to me and walked out and around the city for more than five hours thinking, crying, and asking myself many questions about my life. Why did my mother feel this was better than me? My prayer was that I would never see them anymore. New York City, here I come. I had no idea what was to become of my life after that summer ended.

I had the time of my life that summer. My family wanted me to see they loved me and for my mother to get herself together so that I could come back home and we could be one big happy family. That idea was great on paper. As I rode the bus back to D.C., I could not help but think to myself, how would we react to one another? Will things change for us or would it be life as usual for she and I? I was also hoping she was not with that man anymore, and if she was, would he be involved in my life?

Because I certainly didn't want him to be in mine. When the bus pulled into the city, I must say it was good to be back home. I wanted to see my friends who I had not spoken with all summer. I was hopeful to get back into church and to see all the wonderful people who I had known all my life. I knew my first priority was my mother. I was so ready to start afresh with her so that we could get back to our normal life.

My family had given me enough cash to spend on a cab and to eat and buy whatever I needed for my trip. When I pulled into the old neighborhood, all those old memories came back and it felt great to be home. I felt like this was going to be something different for me and I thought I was ready for it. I walked up the stairs to our door and knocked but mother was not home. I sat on the stairs and waited for her. After a while, our neighbor opened her door and sees me sitting on the steps and gives me a look like I didn't belong there. I asked had she seen my mother? She then tells me the last thing I expected to hear from her. "Your mother moved in with her boyfriend and his kids on the other side of town." My heart dropped in my socks. This had to be a joke. She didn't even tell me or our family she moved. How could she do this to me? I had not spoken to her all summer but surely she spoke with my aunt and told them. Why would they not tell me this news?

I called them to ask, and they had no idea what I was talking about either. I had never felt so abandoned in my life, and my heart hurt from this news. Life with she and I was still the same, just at a new address with other people involved now. When I pulled in front of the house and got out of the cab, I stood there looking at the house for what seemed like hours. I then heard the basement door open and it was him. I felt like I wanted to throw up. He spoke to me and I spoke back to him. He proceeded to grab my bags and tell me to come in the house. I followed him downstairs, and there she is sitting with two other people. They all seemed happy to meet and see me, except for her. I don't recall her saying anything to me. I was so angry at her. I am not sure if I spoke to her. I do recall me rolling my eyes at her. Mac then takes me upstairs, and there are the boys and their sister Crystal. They speak and I speak back. He then takes me up another set of stairs to what was to become my new room.

This was nothing like what I had grown up with in my life. It had a bed and a dresser with this ugly green paint on the walls that was peeling from the ceiling. He tells me, "This is your room. Make yourself comfortable. The bathroom is next to you." My hate for my mother was at an all-time high now. I was so mad at her. I felt alone, afraid and empty. I sat on the bed and cried myself to sleep. There I stayed all night and the next day. I didn't eat anything for two days. I was so depressed about what was happening around me. Not once did my mother come and check on me to see how I was doing. This was my rock bottom moment in my life. I got dressed and stayed in my room for the rest of the morning. Mac came into my so-called room and told me to come downstairs with the rest of the family. I was afraid to be around these people because I didn't know anything about them. In my eyes this was not my family and I wanted nothing to do with them.

When I came in the living room, the boys started with the Q and A with me. Mac told them to stop asking me so many questions and to leave me alone. My mother never spoke to me once. She did not even look at me. I watched her closely. She seemed to be someone I had never seen before. Then out of nowhere she comes into the room and begins playing with them, smiling, laughing, and kissing them. When she does speak to me, it was cold and nasty, telling me to get up and get her something from the other room. I watched her with Mac. I had never seen her with a man so this was really new. Her relationship with Crystal who called her "Mama" knocked me off my feet. She took her everywhere. If she went shopping, I would get nothing. She would pass them their gifts in front of me and then tell me to put the wrapping in the trash. It was in this moment of my life that I understood the story of Cinderella and her stepsisters. I was now living that fairy tale in living color.

I found Mac to be very rude at times, and he was arrogant, egotistical, pompous, and sexist. He chain smoked Pall Mall cigarettes and he drank Jack Daniels. He would speak to people as if they were on his payroll. He was very direct and blunt with his words. That was odd to me because he didn't work anywhere and I found him to be very lazy. When he wasn't drunk he was another person. Both times when I got sick, it was he who took me to the doctor. He never asked for my help with his sons, like my mother would bark orders at me to help. He would often say, "thank you" and "please" when he wanted me to do something for him. He enrolled me in school in the area and made sure I was up every day. He knew how to talk to me and not at me, and a few times he would correct my mother when she would go too far.

In his own way he would try to make sure I had what I needed. When he came home with that brown bag, I knew all that would change. One day I went to the store for him, and when I came back, my mother was in the room crying. When I asked her what was wrong, she would not say. Even though she could be a bitch to me, she was still my mother. I did not want to see her hurt. I could feel the energy in the house so I went downstairs, and there was another woman crying also. I asked Mac what was wrong with my mother. He then jumped up yelling at me, telling me not to ask him or talk to him like I was grown and to watch my tone. I did not back down. I said to him, "How would you feel if you saw your mother crying and you didn't know why?" I then told him this is not about my tone, even though he may not like what I asked him and the way I asked. He did agree with me. He then told me what happened. The home health aide who cared for the boys had a crush on him. She and my mother got into an argument and he told my mother to shut up. When she didn't, he smacked her. He said my mother quickly slapped him back. She told him, "Don't you put your hands on me." He then said, "I must admit, your mother has a powerful punch and I will never do that again." He then told the lady to go home and not to come back.

It was during this time of my life I began to enjoy drugs more and the people I was around while doing them. Cocaine, acid, marijuana, and lots of drinking. I found that acid was not for me. Cocaine became my main drug choice because it was the thing everyone was doing. To avoid the problems I was having at home, I stayed out as late as I could. If there was a party, I was there. I only stayed at the house to sleep and shower. To my surprise, when I came home from school one day, all of our things were out on the street. I was in complete and utter shock. People in the area were mad and upset that this happened to us. I was mad at my mother and Mac. People were coming up giving my mother and Mac money and business cards for lawyers. Then a news crew came, and we were on the five o'clock news for the entire city to see. This did not help my self-esteem at all. We were taken to a shelter that day not far from our home. The next day, food, money, gift cards, and people from around the city came to see what they could do to help.

This forced Mac to stop drinking, and he along with my mother had to get jobs. This also exposed me. When he was drinking, I could hide my problems from him and come home high and pass out. No one would notice me this way. He didn't like what he saw so he put me out on the streets instead of getting me help. My mother said nothing to me. In fact, she thought I was partly to blame for the problems she was having with Mac. That night I slept on the streets in an apartment building on the floor until it was time to go to school. After school I walked to the area where the men prostitute for money. I used the money to eat and the men's home for shelter and to shower. I was done with God for allowing this to happen to me. I wanted a way out of this mess I was living.

I met a man named Tony who was very rich, who would have sex with me, feed me, and he would buy clothes for me. He would take me any place I needed to go. He often spoke about his religion he practiced. Buddhism. He told me that doing this would change my life for the better and that I should come and try it out. He told me that what I was going through had nothing to do with my mother; it was me. Life was about cause and effect. I was getting the effects of everything I had put out in the universe. If I chanted these words, "Nam Myoho Renge Kyo," I would see a complete change in my life for the better. I told him I would give it a try. He took me to this temple where I took part in this ceremony and became a Buddhist for Nichiren Buddhism for America.

After the ceremony, people of all races came to me congratulating me. Many of them told me that if I needed anything to just reach out to them and they would make sure it would be taken care of. One of Tony's friends was a professor at UDC, and he was having a get-together that night at his home. He made sure I knew I was more than welcome to come. His name was Reggie Jenkins. He was very smart, kind, and he seemed to be attracted to me, or so I thought. Because I was still in street mode and ready to sell myself, I came on to him, and he quickly stopped me. He told me, while it was clear he was gay, he was not into me like that and that he was also not Tony. He expressed to me that Tony had a bad habit of using his money to buy people and that I should remove myself from that energy. I told him I had no place to go and Tony was all I had. He offered me a room in his home that night, and that would be my last time ever selling my body to perverted men.

Reggie made sure I got back into school and that I ate and was clean. More importantly, he wanted me to get my mind together and rethink my life and the road I was on. Like Mac, when he drank, he became a completely different person. Unlike Mac, he wasn't rude. He just spoke the truth no matter how raw it was. Things were not good with he and I when he had other gentlemen callers over to see him. They looked at him strange when they saw me. He would eventually call social services to cover himself so that he would not be viewed as a pedophile. Once again I was off to another group home for boys. Once again my mother did not want anything to do with me. I was embarrassed and depressed about my life almost all of the time. However, this time things were very different than the last time. Reggie was still very much a part of my life, and he viewed me as his son.

Reggie eventually met my mother and her new family. He could not understand why things were the way they were for me. He would often tell me my mother was dealing with some issues that had nothing to do with me. He encouraged me to never stop giving up on her and to love her past her hurt. He also challenged me to break the cycle that I saw myself in by fighting to become a better me. He would tell me that I had the power in me to direct the path for my life and that I could live what I dreamt for me. My search for self-love was a never-ending journey that forced me to deal with my pain. Somehow I managed to get back into Reggie's home. I could see Reggie was dealing with his own pain. I later found out it was because of AIDS that was in the news and killing many of his friends. I could see his spirit was shifting and he was not the happy person I knew. He told me that it was time to follow his heart and to do what he felt was necessary for him to grow. So he took a job in Atlanta at Clark University teaching English.

He had a party to say goodbye to all of his friends in D.C., and the next night we went to dinner. When we got to dinner I could feel there was something deeper than his move he needed to express to me. He told me he had AIDS. I lost it, but he kept his cool the entire time. He told me that this was his path and that he was fine with it. He was a man who lived life on his own terms and he had not one regret.

Many years later I was told he moved back to D.C. and that he was not doing well. I found his address so I went to visit him. His mother happened to be in town with him taking care of him. When she opened the door, she looked so drained and tired. She told me he was asleep but I was more than welcome to come visit him. Chances are he would not wake up but I could sit with him. When I walked in his room, he was so thin. My heart broke into a million pieces. His mother sat with us talking to me. I could not tell you anything she said, but I kept it together for her and gave her my ear to say whatever she wanted to say. I could see she needed help so I asked her was there anything I could do for her. She said, yes, could I help change his diaper and clean him up. I could not help but think about this elderly woman having to be here to take care of her son; it should be the other way around, so I was more than glad to assist her. Before I left her I prayed for peace in the home. I looked at Reggie one last time because I knew it would be the last time I would see him. As I sat in my car, I cried for him and for her. Two weeks later he passed.

Life during this time for me was a big blur. I was still very much into drugs and doing absolutely nothing with my life, so I decided that I would honor Reggie and get my GED. I enrolled in a program at UDC that he once told me about. Because of him I was able to get in with no problem. However, I felt like it was not enough and that something was still missing. Then it hit me, I needed to get out of D.C. I knew that If I didn't, I would die in the streets or become a drug addict or both.

I was now back at home with my mother and Mac. I had become very close to the boys. In fact, I love them like brothers. Like everything else in my life, our happy times would not last for very long. Things took a turn for the worse for my mother and Mac. His drinking and smoking caused him to have Stage IV cancer. He was in and out of the hospital for a few weeks. His last visit he never came back home. This was my first time ever seeing my mother broken hearted. Her pain was so deep and real she became withdrawn from everything in life. Crystal's mother came and took her not long after that. A few months later, one of the boys got very sick and he passed away. His mother later told me that he was hollering my name the entire time he was transitioning, wanting me to come help him. When she got up to call me so that I could speak to him, he closed his eyes and he was gone. I was now in the fight of my life. I had no idea if I would survive it. I only knew how to do a few things well: drugs, drinking, and praying. My prayer was very simple. "Lord, teach me how to fight so that I can live to tell my story." Before I could do that, I had some more drama to get out of my system. Until that happened I would stay high.

CHAPTER SEVEN

"Lost And Found"

Before you can begin to love yourself, you must learn to like who you are. Then you must be willing to trust the process.

Most people go through life lost and they have no clue how to come out of the darkness that has kept them in bondage. When drugs and/or alcohol are involved in their lives, this way of living becomes their sole purpose for living. Looking for their next high to try to top the last high is almost always the goal. An addict is not just addicted to drugs or alcohol. They are addicted to numbing the reason they became an addict. I believe that a functioning addict may be worse than someone who is openly using. These people become addicted to a lifestyle of trying to cover up their lies and addiction. It becomes a game in the way they do everything. Not only do they play Russian roulette with their lives, they play it with others' as well. Deep in their hearts they want to be exposed. They desperately want the help that is needed to find their inner strength. But the addiction keeps them hostage to their hidden pain.

When you live in addiction for so long, you forget what it's like to not be addicted. For many addicts they are so far gone, they simply can't find their way out of the darkness. They become accustomed to living life with blinders on, and they settle with where they are in that season of their life. In order to be found, you must admit that you are lost and you need a way out. When you commit to this way of thinking, you must be willing to learn to have the courage to stand in your truth and allow those who love you the opportunity to expose the hurt you have caused in every area of your life as well as theirs. This process is not easy but it is necessary.

It seemed like everything that I loved had died and my life was falling apart at the seams. As much as I would like to say that my mother was not trying to love me, I made it hard for her to do that. I had so much backed up resentment in my heart for her. I played a big part in showing her she could not trust what I said or did. It was during this point in my life that I was most out of control. I would push her and anyone else away who tried to nurture me. Anyone who would try to show love to me was out of the question during this time, even God.

My love was cocaine and drinking dark liquor. People who supplied me with either one got what they wanted from me. If sex was involved, it was a party. To support my habits I had become a thief of any and everything I could get my hands on. I became very creative at how to steal from family, friends, co-workers, and especially my mother. While living with her I would take care of the boys during the day and party at night. Before she got up one morning to go to work, I had gone into her wallet and took all her cash. I threw the wallet in the street so that she would think she lost it. I did this in front of the boys so they saw everything. When she accused me of taking it, I argued with her and cried fake tears because she blamed me. She turned and asked the boys did I take it. I was standing behind her shaking my head telling them to say I didn't do it.

I was so controlling of the boys. I manipulated them into lying for me so many times by rewarding them with candy. I am sure it confused them but they loved me so much they would do anything for me. I was such a jerk to her and to them, for that matter, but I didn't care. My goal was to get as high as I could and stay that way. After Mac's death, he made sure my mother was well taken care of. I looked in the back of her checkbook and took a check out and wrote it to myself for a thousand dollars. When I gave the check to the teller, I then turned on the charm. Because it was such a large amount, they had to call and verify it was legit. Looking back I must have looked like a drug head, so of course they would turn me away. When I got home, my mother was waiting for me and we argued about that for hours. I made up a lie telling her I owed a drug dealer some money and if I didn't pay him back, he would hurt me. She did not fall for it so I called her every name I could think of to throw her off the topic.

The sad thing was, the next day was my birthday. I had no idea she brought me a TV and some clothes. I felt so bad about it for a second. I took the TV to a pawn shop and used the money to blaze up as high as I could get. Happy Birthday to me, you jerk. I had become great friends, if that was possible for me, with a guy who lived in the area named Carl. He lived in the basement of his sister's house. He was always welcoming to anyone who needed a place to stay. We would drink and party with each other, get drunk, and pass out. One day, while me and another get-high buddy were thinking of ways to get money for drugs, I got this bright idea to break into the basement of Carl's and steal his stereo equipment.

I knocked on his door just to make sure it was safe. When he didn't answer, I then went into the window in the back of the house. When I got in, I called him at work to make sure he would not be home any time soon. I ate his food, drank his alcohol, and even took a nap. When I got up I put his stereo into a wheelbarrow and rolled it down the street looking like a real crackhead. When it became too heavy for me to go any further, I hid it in this abandoned garage. I then went to get a friend's car so that I could take it to the pawn shop for money. When I got back to retrieve the system, it was gone.

I had a way of telling on myself without saying I did things that were stupid. I saw Carl one day and brought up this stupid idea of making a mixed tape for something. To this day I have no idea what I said to him. I do recall the look on his face. "It was you" was in his eyes. He looked at me like I was crazy and rolled his eyes. I was so dumb. That night after seeing him, I went home early and took a bath. When I saw myself in the mirror, I broke down and cried. I was trying to make a change for the better for me. I just did not have a clue how to fix the mess I was in. I stopped doing cocaine but began smoking marijuana, a lot of it. I also got a job at a local bar as a bar back. The thing I loved most about working there was I could drink for free. Also all the drug dealers hung out at this spot.

One day I was off so I went for happy hour at the bar. All seemed to be going well this day, almost too well. People were talking, laughing, and a having a good time. I noticed this dark- skinned brother walking into the bar. He orders a drink and makes eye contact with someone he seemed to know at the other end of the bar. He then makes his way towards the guy and they have small talk that turns into a war of words. The next thing I knew he pulls out a knife and he cuts the guy's throat. Blood is everywhere. People are screaming and running away from the blood. The guy then drops the knife and tries to run away, when some of the other people hold him down. It seems as if everything was in slow motion. I walked to the gentleman on the floor and talked to him. I remember telling him it would be ok and to hold on. I placed his head in my lap. The bartenders hand me some rags so that I could cover his throat.

I had his hand in my other hand talking to him. He was giving me eye contact responding to everything I was saying. I could see he wanted to sleep but I kept telling him to stay with me. He is speaking with his eyes but his grip is getting lighter. I began to yell, "GET THE AMBULANCE!" People are asking me, "Is he OK?" I was telling them yes. Within a few seconds, he was gone, but I still kept telling everyone he was OK. When the paramedics arrived I told him to bend down, and I whispered to him, "He's gone." The paramedics looked at me and told me to keep calm. They took over and placed him on a gurney. When I stood up, I noticed that I was covered with blood, and I panicked. I then looked at the bartender, and I could see on her face how I must have looked. She pours a shot for her then she gives me a shot. The DJ then grabs my hand and takes me to the restroom, and he is cleaning me up from all of the blood while I am crying uncontrollably. I could not speak to say anything. All I could do is cry. He then wipes my face. By this time my friends are holding me up and walking me outside to get some air. I don't know what was said to me or who took me home. I don't even recall the next few days. I only remember that it was a sign from God. Oddly enough, when I think about that day, I think about him laying his head on my lap. And I also think of the guy with the knife. I see my face in both of them.

A few weeks later the DJ told me he had been in communication with the deceased gentleman's family. He told them what I had done and how I was broken up about it. They were so moved by my actions that they wanted to meet me. I could not face them nor could I talk about it. I really don't have any regret in life. I do regret not taking the time to meet his mother and father to give them the closure to their son's death. I had blocked it out of my mind, along with so many others things. I remember calling my mother to tell her what happened to the young man and what I had done. She was very quiet until I was done speaking. Before she said anything, I told her I had to get off the phone. She stopped me and told me to be careful. I was her only son. What I heard was, "I love you." My life was never the same after that, and I knew I needed to change something. The problem was I had no clue what, when, or how to change it. What I knew for sure was, if I didn't make a change in my life, I would be next in the morgue or in jail. And that, for me, was not an option.

CHAPTER EIGHT

"Future And A Hope"

For I know the plans for you, declares the Lord, plans for welfare and not evil, to give you a future and a hope .

Jeremiah 29:11

During this time of my life I felt most empty. I felt like I had ran the race that was meant for me to run and I was done. I knew it was time for me to grow up and make some changes that would be best for me or I would die. The clubs, the streets, the drugs, and the sex were all taking their toll on me. I could smell my death. I envisioned my funeral. I hated the way I was seeing myself. Many of the people I was hanging with were in jail, dead, or strung out on drugs. I had chosen to not allow my life to end that way. I felt old, like I had lived my life a thousand times over. I was only 19 years old. I could not continue to live the lie I was living. I asked God to give me a way out, to show me a sign, to make it all go away.

I was still working in the night club, and my choice of drugs was still smoking weed. In those days we called them white boys. "Blunts" came later. Marijuana made me do two things: eat and think. I did a lot of both of them all the time. One night while in the club on a night off, I began talking to these two guys from Norfolk, Virginia, named James and Rudy. We struck up a conversation for most of the night laughing and talking about life. When the bar closed we got something to eat and walked around the city until it was almost morning. I felt like I was a new person with them and I was living outside of what I was accustomed to living. They dropped me off at home. We exchanged numbers and talked for most of the summer. A new friendship had begun mostly with James, and for the first time I knew no sex or drugs would be involved.

I later learned he was in the Navy and had a roommate. While talking one day telling him about my life and how much I hated being in D.C., James says to me, "You should move here with me. You can stay as long as you want." I didn't have to think about it long at all. I told him I would need two weeks to get myself together and that I would let him know for sure what day I would be there. In that one moment in time everything about my life changed. I began to see a new me and I was liking what I saw. There was a light at the end of the tunnel for me. I began to walk towards the light. I had no idea how I would tell my mother, friends, and co-workers, but I was more than ready to tell them. I told my best friend at the time who kept a level head with everything. He didn't do drugs nor was he someone who threw anything in my face about my life choices. He seemed to take it hard but he knew it was the best thing for me.

Pete Caughman and I stayed friends until his death in 2002. It was Pete who would tell me my life was more than what I thought it was. He would tell me if I did not get my life together, that I would die from my own toxic ways. He paid for my ticket to Norfolk, and he would send me money until I got on my feet. Next, I told my co-workers at the bar. I now look back and ask myself, why would I tell them anything? They were all a bunch of shady drug heads whose only concern was getting me high my last night in town which, by the way, I did. When I told them I was leaving, I will never forget one of the guys saying to me, "Who do you owe money to? All you're doing is running from something that will catch up with you sooner or later in life." Why did he say that? Next thing I knew, we were fighting each other while the bartenders were laughing at us looking like two fools. Next, I told my mother. I can recall me feeling almost sick to my stomach just thinking about what she would say. I wasn't sure what she would say or how she would react to the news about my move. I guess I felt that way because any time in my life when I shared what was important to me with her, she would never show me any emotions.

In my head I needed her to fight for me. In my heart I wanted her to love me. I wanted her to tell me not to go; that she needed me and wanted me to stay. I so badly wanted her to validate me and to make me feel worthy of her love. I called her to tell her I wanted to talk to her about something. She said, "Sure, come over," so that we could sit down. She also had something to share with me that was important to her. When I got to her house I was shaking so badly I had to sit on my hands because of the sweat that was coming out of them. As I began to tell her my reason for wanting to speak to her, I could feel the tears coming down my face and I didn't know it.

I could see she was concerned for me. It was my first time ever seeing this look on her face. I told her it was time that I moved and I was leaving the city to move to Norfolk, Virginia. She asked all the right questions. Who do you know there? Why are you moving? What made me want to move to Norfolk? I answered all her question as honest as I could. I didn't realize I was speaking to her with my head down. When I looked up at her face into her eyes, they were filling up with tears. That look gave me everything I needed from my mother in that moment. We spent the rest of the night talking about family and church stuff. She then asked me to stay the night with her before I moved so we could spend my last night in D.C. together. This was a side of her I had never seen before and a part of me felt it was too late, but I stayed.

That night I couldn't sleep. I tossed and turned all night. The next morning when I came downstairs, my mother was sitting at the table waiting for me. I could see she wasn't able to sleep either. I was filled with emotion and once again tears were flowing. She stood up and gave me a hug, and it felt like it would last for hours. It was as if she didn't want to let me go. She then told me I was always welcome home. That love she showed me carried me for the next few years of my life. It was a moment in time that has stayed with me for a lifetime. However, it would take more than that for me to learn how to forgive her. As she walked me to the door, she told me she was sending the other two boys to live with their biological mother. I guess we both wanted a fresh start with life.

I still can recall the bus ride to Norfolk. It was as if I was coming out of the darkness into the light. My life was flashing before my eyes as I watched the trees and scenery of America transport me from the old into my new normal. It was the greatest faith walk of my life at that time. I was looking forward to what was coming my way. In my head I had one major problem that followed me: my addiction to drugs, sex, and drinking. Would I be able to shake it off or would I allow myself to reach for what was purposed for me? Walking into the unknown always felt like the worst thing that would happen in my life. It felt that way for me because living a lie was all I ever knew. In my heart for some reason I knew I would be just fine, but my flesh was in my head telling me I would fall flat on my face and a part of me believed it.

My time in Norfolk was my coming out, living wild and free without judgment or a care in the world. While drugs were not as much a part of my life, they still were very much in my life. The difference between my life in Norfolk and my life in Washington D.C. as it pertains to my addictions was that I was starting to make the choice of doing what I wanted to do. I wasn't doing it to suppress the pain that I had been living with. No one knew anything about what I had endured in Washington, D.C. So I placed all of that pain and emotion in Pandora's Box where it stayed for the next 20 years. My time and life in Norfolk catapulted me into my manhood. There were no restrictions. There were no limitations. There was no one to report to. It was just me and God. The next 12 years of my life in Norfolk would be a rollercoaster of emotions. While there would be some pitfalls and valleys, there were also many peaks.

My time in Norfolk would require me to write a part two to this book because I could not possibly fit all that needs to be said into this book or this chapter.

I was forced to correct a lot of my mistakes and live my truth in front of people who would call me out on my shit. My time in Norfolk, Virginia, prepared me for the greatest spiritual growth of my life that would help me transition into Richmond, Virginia. My time in Richmond would be the place where I would learn to give my whole heart, body, mind, spirit, and soul to Christ. It is where I would seek out my purpose and my calling. It would be where my journey to my purpose would begin. It would be where my hope would become my reality. I found that when you're on your path to your truth everyone can't go with you. I was forced to leave many of my so-called friends behind because I quickly learned they were a major distraction. Your friends in your life should be a reflection of who you are and not a distraction to who you are becoming. Anyone who is a distraction should be eliminated immediately.

My friends in Richmond became family for life and it would be these people who would challenge me more than anyone. They would do it without being judgmental of me, and they would love me, flaws and all. I would have to renew my mind by learning to love every inch of me by eliminating every toxic person from my past. I would have to embrace what was to come even though I had no clue what was coming. Most of the men in my life who had their mothers showed me how to honor my mother. The love I saw in them that they showed to their mothers was inspiring to me. Although I saw it, I could not gather in my head the concept or the idea as to how to give my mother the love I so badly wanted to give her. I pleaded with God to help me renew my mind. He gave me exactly what I asked for, and then the work began for me.

This work happened in three phases for me and they were all spiritual and they would all become the foundation in my spiritual walk. Everything I was taught as a child had to be separated into two parts: what worked for me, and what didn't work for me. What I learned is that what worked was that I could not settle. I had to step into some crazy faith and trust the God in me. Lastly, I had to be able to recognize God's voice. To do this, I had to get centered and locate a church that would nurture my spirit man for growth.

A friend asked me to visit his church in the historic part of town. I had begun to see the change in him so I was willing to go and see what he was being fed. As we walked to the building, I got the same feeling I got as a child walking into Union Temple. The service was beyond amazing. It was what my spirit needed to press to the next level in my faith walk. Victory Tabernacle Baptist Church was my new normal.

I clearly heard the voice of God speaking to me, and He was not kind in telling me about myself. It would be the hardest fight of my life between me and God. I hit many walls during this season of my life because I could not see the lessons. I was what you would call a repeat offender. The toughest part was to surrender. Eventually I had to strip down every layer, one by one, and I hated every minute of it.

The first layer showed me that I was very selfish. When you become addicted to drugs and alcohol, you become so wrapped up into self you have no concept of other people's feelings. I began to think like most people do and say that God knows my heart and what I went through; he understands my hurt. While this may be true, He still needs to hear from you as to what you need from Him so that He may be effective in helping you overcome your problems. Not only did I think this, I also thought because He knows my pain, I get a pass. I was totally trying to play God for a fool. I just was not getting it at all and that was because of my ego. I kept hitting many walls over and over again or, in my case, God was slapping me upside my head. Until you learn the lesson that life is trying to teach you, you will continue to repeat the same lessons.

I became very active in "Victory." While in church one Sunday Bishop Kevin J. Harris asked the members to help with one of the ministries in the church called The Fish and Loaf Ministry. This was a feeding ministry that would feed hundreds of people in the Richmond area once a week. I quickly raised my hand and was pointed in the direction of one of the overseers of the ministry, Sister Watson.

Sister Watson became my angel on earth who God strategically placed in my life at the right time. She has always shown me nothing but love. She always obeys the voice of God when He speaks to her. I first saw her boldness in the grocery store one day when she told a complete stranger what she saw in her life. She has great courage when it comes to speaking truth to others. She asked me about my mother one day. When she did, tears came streaming down my face, without me saying anything. She knew I was struggling in that area. When I told her I had not spoken to her in many years, she said to me with boldness and authority, looking me directly in my eyes, "All God wants is for you to honor her. That's it. He will do the rest."

When she said it, I got a bit defensive and began to tell her about the way my mother treated me growing up. All the pain I had pushed down was coming up out of my flesh. She was having none of it and without any hesitation said to me, "So she is just your mother, not God. You are not perfect yourself. Why are you expecting more from her than what you are willing to give?" I was speechless. I knew she was right. I took a deep breath and said, "You are correct." She said it one more time. "Call your mother before it is too late." I told her I was not ready now but I would. "All God wants is a yes." She didn't push it any further. She told me, "Now I know how to pray for you."

I felt her prayers daily and I began to pray for her in return. We became family. We even discovered that her husband had some people in his family from Virginia with the same last name as my family. More importantly, I watched her serve with excellence and grace in everything she did. She always said yes whenever asked to do anything for the church. I would become her righthand man, cooking, cleaning, shopping, serving. And anything else that was needed we did, many times spending money out of our own pockets for the ministry.

During this time I was asked to work as a coordinator for the Tim Reed Foundation. They had a yearly scholarship fundraiser for HBC schools. This year they were having it in Richmond. I played a big part in the event and I must say my ego got too big for my head. When they gave us free passes for family and friends, I gave everyone a ticket who did nothing for me just so that I could impress them. The one person who should have gotten a ticket I didn't think about until it was over and too late. God slapped me hard during that season and I felt it. I was so embarrassed and ashamed of my actions that the guilt ate me up inside.

Stacey never changed how she treated me. She never stopped loving me. In fact, she loved me harder. This was my selfish lesson. God never blesses selfish people or rewards them openly. Service has nothing to do with what you can do to be seen. It's about what you can do for others so that their dim light can shine brighter than yours. Sister Watson is one of my greatest heroes.

Bishop Harris truly operated in the five-fold ministry. I was most moved when I saw him in worship. It pushed me to elevate my worship time. His heart was always about the people in the community and the Richmond area. But deeper than any of those things, he honored his mother openly for all to see. He was a man of few words outside of the pulpit. When it came to his mother he was very vocal about what she meant to him, and his expression of devotion to her inspired me. In my mind any man who lived his life with the level of integrity that he did, I had great respect for.

His knowledge of the Word was impressive and he preached with confidence. One Sunday he spoke into my life so eloquently I knew it was God. It was as if he was inside my head saying verbally what I was thinking. He was so on point that it scared me. "God wants you to forgive with your heart so He can heal your mind." He then said, "God wants to use you for His Kingdom. There's a book inside of you, but it can't be released until He can trust you." I had never shared that with anyone, and he was correct. My heart was so damaged. I didn't have a clue how to forgive so that I could do the work needed for my community. I could do one thing that I couldn't do before, hear the voice of God. Because of that word spoken to me, I cried all day. I knew it was God speaking clearly to me, and my body felt refreshed.

I felt for the first time in my adult life that my walk with God was pleasing to Him. I thought to myself, *I need to be like David and write down my visions for my life.* I had great work to do but I was still not ready or was I willing. I was still secretly dealing with my pain from my youth. I knew in order for me to move forward I had to shift. While I had no clue how to shift, I was encouraged to move. I was willing to take the hits along the way. No one grows in life without taking some major hits. These hits are only there to build up your courage to strengthen you for what's to come next.

The more I served others, my faith was building daily. I was becoming a new person that I had never seen before. Sister Watson was pushing me to minister to the men coming in the doors. I would pray with them and for them. God was using me to speak into their lives. We were truly ministering to broken people who were in need of much more need than food. I quickly learned that if I was going to pray and touch and agree with others, I would have to be about our Father's work. I would have to live what I was saying to others.

My spirit man was gaining strength and my mind was being renewed because of it. One day while setting up to feed the people, Bishop came from out of his office and pulled me aside to tell me to expect a call from someone that would elevate my strength. The next day I received a call from my mother. We talked on the phone for more than three hours non-stop. She was talking to me and not at me. She was so open, I could feel her spirit speaking to my spirit on another level. Before we hung up from one another, she said three words I had waited my whole life to hear, "I LOVE YOU." Not only did she say it but I felt it. I knew it was real. There was a future and a hope for us that I had never experienced in my life. I was being renewed, and I could feel God shifting me to another level.

CHAPTER NINE

"God Loves Me"

*When you have nothing left but God, that's when you discover
God's love was always enough.*

What I know for sure is that God's love for me has superseded any
kind of love that I have ever known in my entire life. Because of His
never-ending compassion for me, I have a standard of what love looks like
and feels like. I have made it a requirement as to how I receive it and how
I distribute it to those who are in my life. This kind of love is at a level
that is beyond anything I have ever felt I was worthy of. My valued life
is validated daily because of this knowledge I have obtained. The work it
has taken me to understand that, not only am I worthy of God's love but I
deserve it, I had to go to a deep place in the center of my core to reach the
foundation of what I didn't know or ever thought existed. What I found
was this amazing gift from God that we call Spirit. When I realized that
my spirit was created from the DNA of God's spirit it all made sense.

How could I love me and not love God, or how could I love God and
not love me? We are both one and the same, intertwined in the same spirit.
His love for me is the best high I have ever had, better than any sexual
feeling or orgasm I have ever achieved, and more important to me than
what anyone thinks of me. I found that I felt His love most when I see
the smile on a baby who I made laugh,. When words that came out of my
mouth encouraged someone and liberated their souls. When my prayers
became a tool to pray for others and not me. When I removed myself out

of the equation to put others on the level I saw in them that they didn't see in their self. I felt His love moving in me and it was and is totally amazing.

God's love became my new high and I was trying to become addicted to it. The best thing out of all of this that I discovered was, "God loves me just because." Knowing this pushed me to want to serve others the best way I knew how. From my heart. The more I served with Stacey in the feeding ministry, the more God's Spirit connected deeply in my heart. It seemed that everything I asked for in my mind, God exposed it to people who spoke it into existence. These people were building me up and setting me up for my next level into my purpose that I truly did not see coming.

One Sunday, one of the Elders in our church asked me for a ride home, and I was more than glad to give her a ride. When we got to my car, she looked at it and these words she said that I will never forget: "What are you doing in this little car? God is getting ready to bless you with a new truck." In my mind, I was not looking for a new car or the car payment that came with it. I was perfectly happy with my car and no car note. I said to her, " I am not looking to buy a new car. I'm happy with what I have." She didn't miss a beat with her words. "I don't care what you are happy with. God needs you to have a truck so that you can use it for ministry."

The next week I took my car in for a recall on a part that the Saturn dealer would fix for free. I told them I also would like an oil change as well, and anything else that needed to be done, they should do it. While they were fixing my car, a dealer came and asked would I be willing to look at a new car. I said with a smart tone, "Sure, I'm looking at a lot full of them now." I told him, "I have no money to put down. I am not able to make a payment this month or next month. If you could make that happen I'll pick a car out." He told me to go pick out what I liked on the lot. I saw this black fully loaded Saturn Vue that I liked. I told God, if this is for me, then make it happen. If not, I'm still happy with what I have. The sales person came back and told me it was a deal. I let out the biggest scream in that dealership. It was so loud that people began to clap. As I was driving home, I began to think about the words of the Elder I had taken home that Sunday. She was spot on.

We used that truck for everything in that season of my life for the feeding ministry. God was showing Himself to me, and I wanted more of Him. I began doing whatever it took to fill myself up with the spirit.

Reading was and has always been the greatest gift my mother gave me that I felt I benefited from. During this season it was Dr. Maya Angelou who encouraged me most. Oprah had her on her show talking about her book "Heart of a Woman." It was Oprah's book club pick. I knew of her because I remembered my mother reading her book "I Know Why the Caged Bird Sings." I was so moved by this book I could not put it down. But more importantly it spoke to my heart. When I was done reading it, I cried openly to God. It was as if every page I read showed me my mother's heart. I am sure five years or more had gone by since I had last spoken to her. I was so convicted in my spirit for not talking to her, but I just didn't know how to forgive her. I asked God for help in this area of my life. In my quiet time I told God I needed her to make the first move. While sitting at home one evening, my phone rang. It was my mother. She wanted to know why I had not called her. She asked had she done something that caused me to not want to speak to her. I didn't have the courage to tell her, so I said no, and I apologized to her for not reaching out like I should have.

We spoke on the phone that night for almost three hours. When it was time to hang up she told me she loved me. I felt it and I said, I love you back. God was showing me He loved me and He heard every one of my prayers. My worship time with God had changed during this season of my life. It was more personal and deeper, and it was a release like I had never felt before. I was really proud of myself during this season. I would go for long walks and just think, pray, cry, and mediate for hours. My spiritual walk with Christ was shifting in a major way. I wanted to be a vessel for Christ but I wasn't ready yet for the level I needed to be. I can recall me begging God to allow me to preach. He would tell me I was not able to handle that anointing yet but hold on, my time was coming. I still had some growing to do in my mind for Kingdom building.

One of the reasons was, I was one way at church and another way at work and in the world. While I never crossed the lines, I knew God was testing me to see if I would honor Him when He told me to speak. I always failed miserably because of fear. In front of my co-workers and friends I would show my thanks for life; however, I made it about me. My EGO was still a hot mess, but this time I was playing with God. Unlike the other times in my life where I didn't see my mess, I saw my shortcomings and I worked on it so that I would not be a hypocrite in the eyes of God.

I was using that time to write whenever I felt led to write. I kept a journal on me, and when I felt the need to say something, I wrote it down. It was during this season of my life God was using me to prepare for His book that I was about to birth out.

It would be another 20 years but it was coming in God's perfect timing. I would first have to embrace my Yes with a celebration and crush my No under my feet. While on Vacation in San Juan, Puerto Rico, walking on the beach, I had a real moment with Holy Spirit. I had never truly thanked Him for showing me His love. In that moment, I checked my EGO. I made a vow to God that I would honor Him with my Yes. I knew the only way it would be effective was for me to make a change that would shift me from all that was so familiar to me. I had to step out of my comfort zone and shake my foundation that was keeping me afloat. I had to do a major shift in my life and tell God yes to His will for me. The next thing I knew, I was moving across the country to a place I knew nothing about. I leaped into my new normal completely blind. Dallas, Texas, here I come. I had no idea what I was doing, but one thing's for sure, I knew I was walking into my purpose.

CHAPTER TEN

"Purpose Revealed"

What once was a Life lived in Black and
White is now a Life lived in full color.

Most people in society go through life not really understanding who they are and what they are called to do. What they know is, get a job, pay your bills, and hope to have a better day than the one they just had. We are taught to live like robots and function by living life in a routine that we see others do. The schools we go to and the careers of most people are not what defines us. Neither does it demonstrate what our true purpose in life is. There have been many top CEOs who have walked away from seven-figure incomes who go to third-world countries and are liberated and free in their minds because they have chosen to walk the path that led them to their purpose. Others have gone to college to obtain their degrees only to realize that they were not following their heart's passion. Many sit and wait for the big reveal to happen to them and when it doesn't, they do what is familiar to them.

I believe that every person who dreamed as a child and understood the emotions that went with it tapped into their true purpose. We may not have known how to put it into words or what to call it. However, what we knew was that it agreed with something in the pit of our spirit. I also believe that it was placed into our memory banks, waiting for us until it was time for us to put it into action to do the necessary work to make it an effective work that flows and agrees with our calling in life. When we see people like Mother Theresa, Malcolm X, Dr. King, or even your school teacher, we see purpose in action.

What we don't know or see is how their purpose was revealed to them and how it agreed with their spirit. What we don't see is the lessons they had to learn and repeat in order to perfect their gifts. When your calling in life is revealed to you, it is truly a feeling that cannot be put into words. You know it because it flows within your life without you forcing it and it happens effortlessly. Even the people who were meant to journey on your path with you will show up with the ability to do what you need, when you need them to do it, and the heart you need from them to make it work. It will fall in place without you having to say anything out loud.

In order to fully understand your true calling in life, you have to know that it won't pay much. The work is hard. And for as many people who believe in you, you will have an equal amount of people who don't. But the reward in the end of it all will supersede your wildest dreams. Your enemies will be the first to point out your flaws. If you don't have the haters and it's too easy for you and you have no problems, nine times out of ten, you are not operating in your calling. When your purpose is revealed to you and you know that it's right in your heart of hearts, your first step in moving towards your calling is to simply say, "yes." Your next step is simply for you to trust the process and enjoy the journey.

I had gone to Texas to visit for a small vacation. While on the plane on my way back home, I clearly heard the voice of God telling me this was the place for my new beginning. So I quickly said yes to God, and my adventure into my new season began. During this season of my life I was telling God to show me a sign if this was what He wanted me to do. When I returned to Richmond, I saw a member of Victory who had become one of my sisters, Minister Dixson. She asked how my trip to Dallas was. I smiled and took a deep breath, and before I could say a word, she said it. "You're moving to Dallas. I see it all on you." I began to laugh at her words and took it as a sign from God that I was doing the correct thing. I felt I was moving not only to Texas, but I was moving into my purpose, whatever that was.

My last month in Richmond was a roller coaster of doubt for me. It seemed like everything I was trying to plan to make this move happen was falling apart. But no matter what, I was going to make this happen if it killed me. And it almost did. I was meeting some friends for a night of dinner, drinks, and fun. While on my way to pick up a few of my friends, this drunk driver ran a red light and hit my truck and drove off. My car rolled over and landed on all four tires. I could not believe I had been hit. When I got myself together, I checked myself to see if I was OK. Then I opened the door and looked at my car. A woman who was behind me in her car saw the whole thing and could not believe I survived it. She kept looking at me as if I was a ghost and she continued asking me how did I feel. When the police officer came to the scene, he asked me if the person in the truck was taken to the hospital. I looked at him and said, "I am the person that was in the truck." He looked at the truck then at me, and all he could say was, "Wow."

Texas was my next stop no matter what, but I needed to see and talk to my mother face-to-face to tell her the news. Because my car was completely damaged, I had to tell her over the phone. For my mother, moving to Richmond was one thing but Texas was another. Over the years, I could drive to D.C. in a matter of two or three hours. But Texas was not in driving distance. Our conversation was a repeat of our talk when I moved to Norfolk. It was long, polite, and almost sad, but it was embraced in love. I told her I was moving the day after Thanksgiving, so I wanted to spend Thanksgiving with her. It was a wonderful time with family and friends, eating and talking about the good old days. I could see that this was no longer my life.

The next morning I got up and had breakfast with my mother. We had the best conversation we had ever had and it was filed with love. I felt protected by a force other than she and I. I felt angels in our presence and I was completely at peace. That protection would cover me from many things that would come into my life once I got to Dallas. When I arrived in Texas, I was so alone and had no friends besides my co-workers. I found a job working at a university as a supervisor for one of the cafeterias in the science building and it was a cultural shock. My entire staff was all Mexican. Many of them did not speak English. So I had to learn how to be crafty with my communication.

I spent most of my time on the bus and train reading books. I must have read a book a week while listening to music. When you have an addiction, drugs always seem to find you, and I was no exception to this rule. This time I stayed away from the hard drugs but I smoked a lot of weed, and most of my paycheck went to the liquor store. I thought I had conquered my need to numb my pain, but the truth was, I had never dealt with it. I just patched it up as I went about my life. My weekends were the happiest time of my life during those days. When I wasn't high or drunk, I was always mad at life. I constantly felt I wasn't good enough. I was longing for something that would catapult me into the place that I was meant to be.

God was trying to detox me from the things my flesh hungered for and my mind thought I needed to move forward. I was in a tug-of-war with my spirit and my flesh. My deepest secrets were holding me hostage at gunpoint trying to stop me from living my purpose. I was drifting towards darkness, away from my light, and this time I had no family or friends to pull me away from the hell I was sinking into. I kept a mask on at all times while at work, on the bus, and with anyone who I came in contact with. I was in an unknown place thinking of a way out of this pain. By this time my purpose was completely gone from my vision and it was out of my reach. I was stuck with no plans for my next level, so I did what I knew how to do best, get high and drunk. But it was not enough.

New Year's Eve 2006. I can't recall how I got to church but I made it. Friendship West was just what my spirit was longing for. I went in empty and left out half full. I returned to my roots, my foundation, my source. My light was on dim but it was not fully lit. I was hearing from God once more. But now I had to be still in silence and not move until I got clarity for what was next. I was willing to give God a "yes," and it felt great, but fear was still in my spirit. My yes was slow but I said it from my heart. I knew that was all God wanted from me was a "yes." I felt a New Nation of believers were on the way to help me birth out my purpose. All I had to do was trust the process and wait. During this time I was having dreams that were so real I would wake up and was not sure if I dreamed it or had I lived it.

This one particular dream I had was very detailed in every way imaginable. I was riding the Dart train system in Dallas on the Red Line going downtown. In the dream I had no reason for going downtown, but I felt whatever it was down there I needed. As I was riding I felt anxious to get there to see or hear what was there for me. I had no stop in mind to get off at so I just kept riding until I felt the need to get off. When I got downtown, I felt compelled to get off at the West End station. This stop downtown is where every bus and train meets. It is the central location for the Dart system and there are people everywhere. This location is the spot I was pulled to get off at. I found myself standing there looking up at the sky as people were walking around me. Then I heard this charismatic voice speaking.

When I turned my head to look for the person speaking, the sun's glare was still in my eyes so I couldn't see where I was going. I just followed the voice. As I approached the voice, there were people standing around listening to what was clearly a man speaking. As I was standing in the back of him, the sun was still blocking my view from seeing his face. But the words that were coming out of his mouth had everyone hypnotized. People were shaking their heads in agreement with what he was saying. There were even a few people crying. He wasn't yelling or being loud, but his words were heartfelt and agreeable. While he was speaking, no one was moving. Then a bell rang and he stopped speaking and began shaking people hands as they walked by him thanking him. I was being pulled to do as the other people were so I reached for his hand. When he turned to me the sun was brighter than ever but I could feel his hand in my hand, and then he said to me, "Thank you for coming. My name is Dexter. God bless you." When I put my hand to my face to block the sun so I could see him, a train came zooming by with a gush of wind. Then I woke up breathing very heavy. But I felt refreshed.

I heard the voice of God speaking to my spirit telling me to remember the voice. During this time I was working at Medical City in Dallas managing a few gift shops in the main building. As I was making my rounds to the other stores in the building, I walked in the baby gift store to see one of the young ladies working there name Brandi. She was playing a CD of someone ministering and it connected to my spirit immediately. I felt like I heard this voice before but I wasn't sure of who it was so I asked her, "Who is that?" She said, "That's my Pastor, Pastor Dexter." I almost passed out when she said his name. That was the voice in my dream, and the name of the person in the dream was Dexter. I told her about my dream, and she and I agreed this was a sign from God. I told her I had to get to her church. There was something there for me.

She gave me a brochure with the church name and information. When

I called the number, a woman answered the phone. We spoke very briefly. When I told the woman about my dream, even she agreed this was a clear sign from God. That Sunday I put on my Sunday best and went to Gospel Tabernacle North. It would soon become New Nation Deliverance Temple, now known as New Nation. When I got there that Sunday, I felt like I was home. I knew that this was the place I was to be at for the perfecting of my purpose. This lesson was the greatest one for me to learn. Always obey the voice that speaks to your spirit, your truth, your heart, and always trust what it tells you. Don't ever be afraid to move, even if you don't know where you are going. My purpose revealed itself to me, and now was the time to embrace all things new.

CHAPTER ELEVEN

"A New Nation"

Transforming Lives to Glorify God - Pastors Chris & Felicia Dexter

Therefore, if anyone is in Christ, he is a new creation. The old has passed away; behold, the new has come. There is a benefit in starting over, starting fresh, and making everything in your life new. What I know for sure is that starting a new life while creating a new normal is not only beneficial for you but for those who are or who have been important in your life and the journey you have been assigned to walk. Creating my new normal for me was so important for my future that I could not just start over in one area of my life. It was important for me to start over in every area of my life. What I discovered most was the way I viewed myself was very critical for me and that I didn't want other people to see me outside of who I was.

I had very low self-esteem and it was a constant struggle for me to rise up to the level of other people's expectations and to be accepted by them. So I learned how to put on a facade and to dream of a better life that allowed me to create this new normal. I soon discovered it was detrimental to my calling in life. What I know for sure is that when you get a new opportunity, you get to create the vision that you see for yourself and not the illusion that you have created. When people create an illusion, it becomes an image of what other people think and how they see you. It has nothing to do with the core of who you are called to be. Starting a new normal for me was very much like going away to college. I had a choice to go away and learn and apply what was given to me through the years; to also create a positive new normal to be effective for others so that a change can not only happen in their minds but also in their spirits. Starting over had nothing to do with me but had everything to do with my purpose and the journey that I was purposed to be on.

I could go one way or I could go the other way and do what I've done before. The drinking, the partying, the drugs, the sexually promiscuous lifestyle that was way too easy to do. I found that no matter what city or country I went to, that lifestyle followed me. I was attracted to people who would literally walk up to me on the streets and ask me was I interested in purchasing drugs or did I want to go to the hot party. I didn't want that attraction to be on my life any more. I wanted the anointing to be infectious, so infectious that when people saw me, they saw something that they couldn't explain. This new normal allowed me to create a new nation not just in a church but in the temple that dwells in me.

When you understand the path that you have been chosen to walk, you understand that you must embrace everything that is around you while walking this time out. It's not about proceeding through life to get to your appointed destination; it's about embracing the sky, the grass, the people, the smell, the air, and the words that people say, the songs that you hear, and the books that are placed in front of you. Everything in life is literally a lesson for you, and if you don't pay attention to the calling and to the still small voice that speaks to you, you will miss your opportunity to meet great people, to see things that will change your life, and to do things that will be forever imprinted in your mind so that it can catapult you into the next level that is purposed for your life.

What I know for sure about life is that when you make the attempt to make a change, you must have a plan. In my plan, what I knew for sure is that I wanted to be a part of a church that didn't practice religion but they practiced a lifestyle of worship. When you make a plan and you have the willingness to pursue your plan, you will always have many options to choose what is perfectly chosen for you. It will fit your calling and there will be no question as to if this is meant for you. Before coming to New Nation Church I had to try on many types of worship experiences until I found the perfect fit for me. I also had to balance my personal life and not allow the freedom that I had to express myself in a negative way while being around toxic people get in the way of my ultimate goal in life. This also included my work.

Many people don't understand, and I was one of them, that your work that you choose should also be an expression of who you are. While I liked my job and I liked the people that I worked with, I just did not feel that it was allowing me to be who I am truly called to be. I knew that I had to find a new pathway in expressing my love for people and teaching them a better way of living. Creating a new nation for who you are called to be is work. Creating a new nation in a land that you know no one is true ministry. Creating a new nation in your life by building a better temple for your soul to dwell in is necessary.

While I was going to New Nation Church I was also going to another well-known church in the Dallas area called Friendship West. I must say that while I did enjoy the word and teaching and the messages, I was still not getting that personal nurturing that my soul needed. Many days I would get up to go to the "wild wild west" as they called it, and for some reason I would end up at New Nation. It just felt like family, and that personal spiritual feeding was being offered to those who were willing to accept it. I was more than willing to accept it. I was hungry for it. It took me almost six months to join New Nation. When I did, I felt completely relaxed and at home.

I got right to work in the ministry, first becoming a member of the Praise Team. I had gotten back to my first love of singing, and we had the best time preparing and presenting to the church on Sunday mornings. Pastor Dexter also put me to work fast by having me lead a few songs. One of the songs he would introduce me to would become my personal testimony for the rest of my Life, a song called "He's Able." I found Pastor to be a great teacher of not only the Word but also his willingness to seek God in everything he did and does.

The greatest lesson I have learned from him, and there have been many, has been the most important foundation for me to stand on in some of my most trying faith walks. "In everything you do, be Spirit led." When he said this principle, it seemed to agree with my soul and I could not and have not let it go. It was as if God wanted those words to be released into the atmosphere for me to receive. This one principle would ignite my fire and unlock years of pain I had buried deep inside my heart. Because of him I became a lover of the Word. I also wanted to learn how he could be so humble all the time. Humility would be the leading principle that would not only allow me to deal with my pain, but it would also teach me how to forgive those who were the cause of it. I would need these two very important lessons in order for me to come out of what was about to change everything in my world in a matter of five minutes. Everything in this book that you have read flashed before my eyes. The only thing that would pull me out are the teachings I had come to know and live and the willingness to sing out loud and boldly, He's Able!

I was working at Medical City Hospital in Dallas, Texas, for about four years, when one day I noticed that I was suffering or, rather, experiencing severe migraine headaches. I didn't think very much of them. I just took a few Tylenol and did the normal things to combat the headache so that I could get through the holidays. We were two days away from Christmas and one day from Christmas Eve, so I was more than excited to wrap up my day and get home to celebrate the birth of Christ with my new church family. A customer came into my store and asked me to reach for something on a shelf that required me to get a step stool. I proceeded to get the step-ladder and go up the ladder to get what she wanted, and the next thing I knew I was out. She caught me before I hit the ground and walked me to the Patient Advocate Care Center where they took my blood pressure and checked my vitals.

I had passed out again, and they rushed me to the emergency room in the hospital. When I woke up there was a team of doctors, nurses, and staff standing around me calling my name. I knew them all quite well because they were regulars in my store that I managed. I was just confused as to why I was on a gurney, why my clothes were off, and why they were all looking at me so seriously. They explained to me that they did a CAT scan and that there was some great concern as to what they found. The CAT scan showed that I had a golf ball figure that was in my head and they needed to do an MRI to make sure that it wouldn't rupture my brain.

I immediately panicked and got scared, but then I pulled it together and commanded everyone in the room to stop what they were doing. They all looked at me, and my request was given to me. I needed my phone. I needed to call my mother. But as I went to dial the number, I heard the Lord say, "No, call your Pastor." I dialed my Pastor's wife's number, Pastor

Felicia, and she picked up on the first ring. As I am telling her what was going on and how I had no clue what to do next, I felt tears welling up in my eyes and my voice begin to choke. She immediately commanded me to stop crying. She said that we're not going to go there, that we were going to trust God; that we were going to come out of this and that we were going to be victorious. She spoke strength into my life. She spoke confidence into my mind, and she spoke peace into my heart. I immediately took a deep breath and told her, okay, I agreed. She then told me that she was going to call Pastor, her husband, and the two of them would be at the hospital to see me.

I then immediately called my Godmother Val Mathews and told her what was going on. As I was on the phone with her, the team in the room told me that they had to move quickly because they were not sure how this was going to turn out for me. The next 30 minutes of my life changed my entire world forever. The doctors told me that the results from the MRI did not look good and that they would have to perform emergency surgery on my brain the next day. I was immediately taken to ICU, and every hour I was in there it seemed I was not getting any better. I began to throw up. I began to have dizzy spells. I began to hallucinate. Pastor and his wife came into the ICU room with me, and they both immediately went into spiritual warfare in that room praying in the Spirit.

We began singing songs of worship. They began to read scriptures. They began to speak over my life, and we all believed that God was going to heal me and that I would come out of this and be victorious. It was something I had never seen before in my life. This was another level of spiritual warfare. The doctors came in and told me that my surgery was scheduled for 12 noon the next day on Christmas Eve. I could not believe what I was going through, but I did believe that I was going to come out and be okay. That night I could not sleep. It was a rough night for me. The next morning a team of doctors came into my room and told me that they had to move my surgery up a few hours because they were concerned about what was going on in my head. If they did not perform the surgery sooner than later, that I would have a brain aneurysm and be paralyzed for the rest of my life, or worse, I would die.

They then began to tell me that the outcome of the surgery could go either way, but the expectations that they had would be that I would be blind in one eye. I would have to learn to walk again. I would have to take speech lessons. I would also have to learn how to use the activity of my limbs to write. The most important thing in their minds was to get me into the operating room to take care of this situation and do it quickly. I was in surgery for six hours, and when they brought me out, they took me back to my ICU room. There were three of my staff members there waiting when I opened my eyes. I saw their faces and I called them each by name and gave them the thumbs up. I saw the tears in their eyes, so that told me that I did not look good. But there was a strength in the pit of my stomach pushing me to get better.

The next few days were crucial for my well-being, so I pushed extremely hard when the therapist came to get me out of bed to walk. I had to literally learn to walk again. That was the hardest part to all of this, trying to walk and being scared that I would fall and hurt myself, not having any control over my body. I got halfway around the corridor and realized that I had to go to the restroom and could not hold it. I urinated on the floor. I felt so defeated. As the staff and the nurses were cheering me on for doing such a good job with my walking, I began to cry because I felt humiliated and I was embarrassed. While in ICU I did my leg lifts while in bed and I stretched my arms. I would walk around the room holding onto the furniture and the bed. I was always alarming the nurses because the alarms would go off every time I would get out of the bed. The next day the team of doctors came in to look at me, and they felt it was best that I would go to a recovery room and do therapy twice a day because they were amazed that in 24 hours I was alert and I was moving so well.

Every day that I was there my pastor came to see me. He even picked up my mother and Valerie from the airport for me. It was my mother's first airplane ride, and she was determined to come see how her child was. I was recovering so rapidly that the doctors were in amazement, and they felt for certain that it was time for me to go home. I had my brain surgery on Christmas Eve, and on New Year's Eve I was in church celebrating the New Year 2008 with my mother and Valerie.

I returned to my doctor for a follow-up appointment the next week, hoping he would congratulate me on my recovery and for not walking with a cane and for being extremely alert, but he had bad news for me. The tumor-like mass had returned and they wanted to go back in and do another operation. I was extremely crushed and upset by this news. I called Pastor to inform him of the news. I could not get the words out without crying. When I told him what the doctors wanted to do, there was a certainty and authority in his voice. He told me, "NO. Do not allow them to operate again. This time we're going to believe God for a miracle." Every week for the next two months I would go to my appointments, and many times I wasn't sure if it was all worth it. One morning before getting ready for my appointment, I had the radio on and the song "He's Able" came on. I began to cry and worship God from my heart, and there was a shifting that happened in me.

I made up my mind that I wanted this to be over and done with. I would completely give it to God and not think about it anymore. A few weeks later my doctor told me that it was completely gone and that they could not find any sign of the mass. I stood in front of the hospital and praised God openly while people walked by looking at me. It was the Miracle that Pastor and I touched and agreed with each other for. After all I had gone through during that season of my life, it was not over for me by any means. There was more learning and pain for me to unearth, and it would come from the most unlikely person.

Pastor Dexter would open up Pandora's box and it was ugly. I was in a Sunday morning service, and I must admit that there was a presence in the sanctuary that day that was undeniable. While sitting there I could feel that there was a major shift that was about to take place in my life. I literally became a bit frightened about what was going to happen. Then Pastor called my name and he said it. He told me in front of the entire congregation that I had nothing to be ashamed about. My molestation that occurred in my youth had nothing to do with me and that it did not define who I was in my adult life. He also told me that my purpose for that season of my life was to operate in forgiveness. I immediately broke down in an uncontrollable sobbing cry for help.

I also was dealing with embarrassment. I felt shame and guilt. I felt guilty that I had never truly dealt with any of those issues that he spoke about and, quite frankly, until he mentioned it, I had not thought about it in more than 40 years. Now the box had been opened and I could not stop thinking about it. And for that reason, I hated him for doing that to me and it catapulted me into depression. Everything that I spoke about in this book (Toxic Waste) that dealt with my molestation as a child was brought back to my memory on that day and for the next two weeks or more, whenever I was alone. Whenever I thought about it, whether in my car, at home, or even at work, I would cry. I cried for many reasons but probably the biggest reason was that I had never truly learned how to forgive.

How can I forgive the people who took advantage of my youth, of my virginity, of my mind, and for raping me of my innocence and for pushing me into the mindset of confusion as it related to this demonic spirit that I lived with daily? On top of all of that, I then had to forgive my pastor for pushing me to another level of forgiveness and encouraging me to forgive while in pain. As much as I hated it, boy, did I have a lot of work to do. Once again, Pastor spent as much one-on- one time as he could with me to help me overcome what had been exposed. As much as I tried to push him away, he fought even harder so that I would not go back into the darkness that I had become accustomed to living in.

What I discovered in that season of my life is that forgiveness is not only liberating for your spirit, but forgiveness is liberating for your mind. It sets you free from all of those obstacles that you have built up, all of those walls that you refuse to knock down, all of the hate that you have embraced. Forgiveness is truly the key to liberating you and catapulting you into your purposed life that God has for you. But you cannot walk in your calling until you truly understand why you are forgiving, why you need to forgive, and how to forgive and how to set it free while never looking back. I have heard many people say that forgiveness is not about the other person but forgiveness is about you. While I find that statement to be true, part of me does think that it is about the other person. Because when you do it for them as well as you, you release the seed that they have planted in you into the atmosphere. You uproot it. You dig down deep, and you discard it so that your foundation that you build your new normal on cannot be tainted by unwanted weeds, debris, trash, or dirt.

Forgiveness allows you to create a new nation of people around you who will encourage you to think, to be, to exist, but more importantly, to operate in your calling by being fully present without any distractions from your past. I learned in that season that we should have solid people in our life to love us through the hurt and pain, who will remind us that we are more than what the oppressor has tried to manifest in our lives. Forgiveness is work that does not happen overnight. It may take some weeks; it may take others months. But for me it took years. Even now I still work on it daily so that I won't allow that spirit to ever overtake all the work I have put into becoming the man I am today.

The next step was for me to embrace my calling, and that was probably the only time I feared the unexpected. My calling involved me helping people, not just on a spiritual level but also in the physical. This calling for me came in two parts. The first part was on a midweek day, Pastor called a meeting for a few members who had expressed their interest in ministry. I happened to be one of them, but I had no idea he was ready to push us to the next level in our calling. For the next seven or eight years, I, along with many others, studied under his leadership in our bi-weekly class for Ministers. Many have fallen and a few have stayed for the perfecting of the Kingdom. I also served as his helpmate and became very active in many other areas of leadership within the church. The other part was the work outside of the church where the need is for the people. I became a peer support counselor for a homeless shelter in downtown Dallas. I then became a vitamins expert teaching people how to live a holistic lifestyle through nutrition and vitamins. I had found my calling, and my purpose was being activated daily.

The people I met were amazing: a cancer survivor, an overweight man with heart problems, a woman with digestion issues, a mother with a child who could not focus, and the list goes on and on. Many of these people became regulars and I was able to reach then on a much needed spiritual level. That is where the work for me began and it continues daily. In my personal life, my relationship with my mother changed drastically. She was a much better mother to me as a man than she was for me growing up. We even talked about the mistakes she made and the one I made on our path to our calling. She was a big part of the research for this book, giving me information and family secrets that had never been exposed. I had never seen or met my biological father, and when I found him, she was so happy for me. She even shared their story with me about how they came in contact with each other. He, on the other hand, would not reply to any of my messages, cards, text messages, or emails.

It was my mother who gave me the encouragement I needed to keep moving and not allow what I didn't have from him to sway me from my goals. My mother became so transparent with me about her life and how she wanted to not be like her father. She understood that because of the seed that he planted, there were many things she just could not avoid. When you live life one step at a time, you honor the journey that you have been chosen to walk. I always say, just breathe and take it all in, and don't lose yourself or think too much of yourself. Stay humble and hungry for what may come.

As for me, I made the choice to follow my heart and be Spirit led in everything I do. I have been asked by many people about how to handle problems that have come up for them. I always listen, ask questions, think before I speak, and I never judge. There have been many times I put myself in their shoes no matter how heinous the act they have done. I do this because we as humans have everything in common that allows us to operate on earth. Other than a few things, we all have a brain, skin that bleeds, a head, body, and a soul, spirit that dwells in us, and the compassion to love or hate. I choose to be a builder of love. I understand that it is my purpose in life to help people build a new nation in their temple. When you teach, you have to be willing to live what you teach. When you give, you have to be willing to give, even when it's not comfortable for you. The biggest thing about life is that you must always be willing to learn and have the courage to be you at all times. I have seen courage in many of the people who I once viewed as weak, mean, or self-centered. I now see them as some of the bravest people I have had the pleasure to know and love. I choose to view their life as a class and learn from them how to be the best me I can possibly be at all times while living life out loud.

CHAPTER TWELVE

"Learning 2 Walk Again"

We walk by faith, not by sight. 2 Corinthians 5:7

Everything that we do in life is an example of what we have learned from what we have seen or heard. We process those things and make them our own in our minds and then they become a part of our psyche. If you are around people who cuss all the time, more than likely that will become a part of your language. If you see people hate and they do nothing when they see an injustice, then that will indicate how you will respond when you see an injustice. Growing up I saw my mother read so I picked that habit up and became a reader. There were also things that I saw and heard that I didn't understand, so I just did it until I saw, heard, and learned better. When you know better, you do better. I believe when you understand your purpose, you fully understand your truth. **The measure of a purposeful life is always lived in Truth**. Your purpose is not what you do but it is who you are. From the moment you were formed in the belly of your mother, you became purpose. Everything else after that was a lesson to set you up for your calling. Learning to walk again is about changing what you saw and heard in life and walking in the calling that lines up with your purpose (who you are).

Nothing in life is perfect, but that doesn't mean you can't keep striving for perfection. In 1846 Antonio Meucci invented the first basic phone. Many years after that, the phone was seen as the greatest invention and it was perfect. Now we know that while it may have been perfect, we now have better phones with many features on them that we can now carry with us. Every year companies keep striving for perfection to outdo what they have already done. When we were babies our parents saw the perfect child in their eyes. As we grow, the goal is to become a better version of our younger self. Perfection is sometimes seen as arrogant or self-centered by many people. I think that perfection is none of these things; the way we express ourselves is. Never allow people to talk you down from climbing the wall of perfection. It is the pathway to your higher self.

Living life on your own terms means you have to do things your way when people are not in agreement with you. In those moments, you must be willing to do things when people turn their backs on you and look the other way. **You can't live because everyone is looking.** You can only live your best life when everyone is not looking at you. When all eyes are on you, you become focused on doing things to please others and not what you were called to do. When a horse has on blinders, it takes the focus off of what is on the sideline and allows the horse to move forward. Your goal in life should be what's in front of you to achieve. You must be willing to live out loud when people want you to be quiet and not make any noise. Always live in the rhythm of life and not man's rhythm.

You are a born winner, baby, so live like you have already won. My good friend and brother Demetrius Butler lives by this motto daily (born winner). He always adds "baby" at the end of it with a laugh. He tells me all the time that "no matter how things may look to people on the other side looking in at my life, how I see myself is the only thing that matters." What that means is, I see myself winning in everything I think or do. Being a winner is in the mind. It's an action. It's how you move when you need to move at the right time, even if it does not work out for you. When people see your failures as a loss, you should see them as a lesson that may need some adjustments. Being a born winner allows you to understand and know in your heart that you were chosen to succeed and not to fail in life. So celebrate your successes and learn from your setbacks.

The one place in the world that I will always find peace at is in my home. **You should always make your home your spiritual sanctuary.** There should always be peace, love, joy, and security where you eat, sleep, and dwell. Never allow negative spirits that people may have enter into your temple. You control the presence of good and evil that comes into your home. I would hope that good energy will be your choice. You should always discern when people are not flowing with the energy that you have in your home. You can never be afraid to speak your truth by telling people to exit your home and take what they brought with them and go. There must always be a spirit of agreement with the people who enter in your house. If not, you must have the courage to stop them at the door or, with some people, on the parking lot. What you read, the music you listen to, what you view on television, and the words that you speak in the atmosphere all play a part in the peace that you live in. There should always be a rhythm that flows with who you are and the peace you carry with you when you enter and exit your dwelling place.

When I decided to move to Texas, it was for what I thought was love. When that didn't work out, I was in trouble. Or so I thought. I had only visited Dallas once, but I felt something pulling me to the city. I knew I had to have courage to pack my things, ship what I wanted, give the rest away to friends, and make the leap into unknown waters. I came to Texas with no job and no plans, only a feeling and a need to make a change for a better life. I was willing, able, and ready to walk into the unknown for my happiness. **You can't be afraid to walk in the unknown.** Fear cannot control your life. If it does, you will fail. Failure cannot be an option when you want to change your life. Sometimes not knowing makes the leap worthwhile. The unknown is a feeling you have in your gut that you can't explain but you know it's working for your good.

I have lived most of my life carrying my past pain in my heart. I found it was a great place to store all the hurt, sadness, anger and bitterness without exposing my true feelings to the people I love. I would go days staying to myself and crying alone until I had no tears to release. I soon learned to store my memories away in what I would call Pandora's box. What I now know is that everything you push down will come up one day to release itself from your stored-up pain. **When your memories become attached to your heart, let them go.** Our hearts are meant for love not storage of those things that block us from growing. You can't grow in life if you don't love with your whole heart. I soon owned my tears and turned them into joy, along with everything else that I allowed to make me think I couldn't grow.

All things in life are lessons that we either grow from, or we repeat the lesson until we get it right. I make it my business to **always move with the flow of life.** I want to encourage you to always follow that inner voice that guides you along your journey to your calling. While you are on that journey, take in everything that is around you and breathe it in. Never allow a moment to pass you without giving thanks for the now. Living in the now means being thankful for making it to the appointed time and space that you are in. Flowing with the rhythm of life is authentic and liberating. It allows you to always live your best life without any apologies. When you get it right the first time, you can count it as a lesson learned.

God always places people in our lives to help perfect us in our calling. It is our job to discern who they are by carefully selecting those who we call family. I once saw a quote that said, "Friends are the family that we get to pick." **We should always center ourselves around people who make up our Super Team of support.** Like any super team, each of your friends should bring something special that adds to your calling and not subtract from who you are called to be. If within your team you are the smartest, brightest, and you have all of the ambition while doing all the work and your team doesn't do even half the work, then these are not the right people for your team. Every person who is a part of your perfecting should first know your heart. If they know your heart then you know without a doubt they have love for you. Love from these people should be a knowing feeling that is based in reaping and sowing, giving and receiving, and never should it be one person that takes all the benefits. These people should always be people who you trust one hundred percent. These people should also possess what I call the Five "C's": Connection, Consistency, Confidence, Commitment, and most importantly Courage. These five things are all rooted in Trust, Love and Wisdom. Wisdom in my opinion is one of the greatest virtues of them all. People with wisdom listen more and talk less. And when they speak, it is done with knowledge and spoken from their heart. When this is done properly and in order, you can receive what is being said with the spirit of agreement. Your super team can be made up of one or five people, as long as you are linked together in agreement. Here's what I know for sure: We were purposed to live in agreement with each other on the planet. That doesn't mean it always works with everyone, but those that it does work with are people who are called to help you shift in life. When we embrace the knowledge, wisdom, love, and the five "C's" that we have for each other in our super team, we then become a force that is unstoppable in life.

When things fail in life, most of the time it's our fault. We blame our mama, our teachers, our friends, and the easiest thing we are so quick to say is, "the devil did it." Stop blaming the devil for your dumb mistakes you make in life. We give him too much credit, and he loves the attention we give to him. **Stay out of your own way and stay focused**. This lesson takes some practice to get right. In fact, it took me years. I had to first look at how I could have done whatever it was I did wrong differently. I had to look at it as a teaching moment. Next, you should always know that nothing in life is a mistake, nothing happens by accident, and nothing that you have messed up is that bad that it can't be fixed. Just relax, breathe, and rethink that problem into your promise. When you are on the right path in life, you should expect something to go wrong. If it doesn't, then how do you learn? When we are focused, we learn from our failures and our wins. What I know for sure is that I became a better me because I got it wrong the first time. Once I got it right, I moved to the next level and prepared myself for the next fight. The Notorious B.I.G. says, "More money, more problems." I say, "The higher you go in life, the harder the obstacles are on the next level."

Learning to walk again is about taking back your purpose that was designed for you to live by God. We are all given our own walk to live, just like we each have our own DNA. No one person is called to do the same thing the same way. There are many principles that we must obey while we walk on the road to our calling. I have given you a few things that I hope will help you navigate through life. I have found that when I allow God to order my steps and **live life one step at a time**, I enjoy the journey, and my calling is more effective for my ministry. The one principle that has helped me the most is to not always think that my walk is always a straight shot forward. There have been unexpected turns, dead-end streets, and many road blocks and detours. However, through it all I have always found my way to my purpose.

Along the way I discovered another principle that has worked for me. I had to learn to ask for help. **If we don't need help, we don't need God.** My faith in God is the only thing that has been the most consistent thing that has always worked. Most of the time when I have been out of order in life, I knew it, and if I may be honest, I was being rebellious. I was this way because of fear of the unknown and what I couldn't control. Once I understood **that faith is about trusting and thinking positive thoughts** about who I am, I soon embraced everything about me that I loved and even those things I didn't like. I have been asked, "How do you embrace what you don't like about you?" Easy. I am honest about me to me. When I look in the mirror, there is no ego, arrogance, judgment, and no disillusion about what I see. I take it all in and I love all of me, flaws and all. Why? Because without a doubt, I know in my heart of hearts that **God loves me** just as I am.

I understand that everything I do in life is a choice. I choose to think of other people the same way as I see myself. **"I am human. I see me in others. I hope for the best in others. I pray for peace in their souls."** My goal in life is for everyone who I come in contact with to know and understand that God loves them as well. To know God's love, we must always surrender and always stay open to receiving what He has for us. We must always look at life as a class and everything around us as a teacher. More importantly, we must be teachable, even when it's uncomfortable. Every chapter, quote, and title in this book was Spirit led. One of the most life- changing principles I have learned from my Pastor Chris Dexter has been the leading factor for everything I do in life. **Always be Spirit led**. This means think with your heart, move when your heart tells you to, and never allow your emotions to control what you do in life, especially when you're upset, moody, bitter, or angry.

It takes great courage to allow a force that you can't see or touch to lead you into the unknown. I have found that when I allow Spirit to lead me, it feels right; I am in agreement with how things turn out; there is no second-guessing myself; and everything falls into place, even those things

I wasn't aware of. One of the lessons I learned from my mother as a child was simple. Always do your best. And what you can't do, allow God to do the rest. Because I know that God is a spirit and I am a spirit connected to flesh, this allows my inner spirit to soar beyond my wildest imagination and grab hold to the Supreme Spirit that allows me to **live out loud** while walking into my purposed calling in life.

"There Remains a Rest"

Yet, but not yet - Rev. Dr. Willie F. Wilson

December 22, 2016

My phone rang at 6:00 am in the morning. When I picked it up to look at it, I could see it was my mother calling so I quickly answered. She was in a state of panic and could hardly get her words together. I told her to calm down and tell me what's wrong. She said to me, "I got out of the bed to go to the bathroom and I fell. I can't walk." I told her to call the ambulance to come get her and go to the hospital. She began to yell and tell me she didn't want to go. She told me she needed me to come home. "You have been gone too long. I need you here." I said to her, "I am in Dallas now. Even if I could get a plane and get to you, you still need to go to the doctor. Promise me you will go." She said, "Yeah, okay," and then hung up on me. I called her back to push her to go. I finally convinced her.

Later that day when I got home from work I called to check on her and she was home. The hospital had sent her back home for some reason. I was not understanding that so I made a few calls to find out what was going on. I have a dear friend who works in this field who put a few calls in and got another story from the Patient Advocate there in Washington and I was in complete shock. When I put in a few more calls to my mother's friends in D.C., they backed up the story from the hospital. Something in my spirit was telling me to go home and check things out for myself. I struggled with going because I felt like I was going into darkness and I was not comfortable with that. I told my spiritual mother Mom Brown I felt like I was going into the wilderness and I needed her to cover me in prayer.

When I got there I could not believe what I was seeing. My mother's home was a mess, unlike anything I had seen from her before. The place smelled of urine. The kitchen was infested with bugs, and I could see mice droppings all over the place. When I walked into her bedroom, she looked like she had aged drastically. I asked her what was it she wanted me to do? She told me she needed clothes folded and her bathroom cleaned and a few other household things that were not important. I stopped her and told her the first thing we are going to do was get her into a hospital to see what was wrong. I sat with her the entire night, and she complained the entire time. She was being so rude to everyone. I also noticed that she was very snappy and bossy to everyone on the staff who was trying to help her.

I could feel myself getting angry so I very calmly told her to think about what she was saying to people and to stop it. I felt like I was correcting a child. It was work the entire time I was there, and we couldn't get much done because it was the Christmas holidays. She stayed in the hospital for a week and a half. While she was there, I cleaned her apartment from top to bottom. I went through her mail and found bills that had not been paid, and some of her important matters that were about to be sent to court for judgments against her. I made calls to fix as much as I could. When I got her home, she took out everything on me, times ten. She called me names that I don't care to repeat and it took me back to my childhood.

After all I had done, it was still not enough for her, and I snapped. I took her walker and threw it across the room and got in her face yelling at the top of my voice, almost to the point I felt my hands getting ready to hit her. It was so bad I was shaking and I wasn't aware that tears were streaming down my face. I then heard the voice of God telling me to "STOP IT NOW." When I did stop, I noticed the look on her face. It was fear. It broke my heart to see her that way. I had never spoken or raised my voice to my mother in my life. I was convicted in my spirit by my actions. I told her I had to leave and get my head together.

I called a friend and told him what happened, and he told me to come to his place to relax. I knew I could not spend another day around her because I was feeling so guilty about my actions. When I got to her place later that night, she locked me out with the chain on the door. I had to wait until she got up out of the bed, and that took her a few minutes to do. When she opened the door, she started it again. I didn't respond back to her. I just took it and went to sleep on the floor. My flight was scheduled to depart at 5:00 pm that day. I was up, packed, and ready to go at 9:00 am. When I walked into her room, I apologized to her and told her that this was not who I was. I had to leave before I hurt someone and get back to my covering that would allow me to get my mind right. I could see on her face that she thought it was my fault and she did nothing wrong, but she did apologize also.

I went to the airport and sat there all day crying and trying to understand what had just happened. When I got back to Dallas I was so depressed I couldn't talk without crying. I was at work one day talking to a customer when she asked me was I okay. The next few months while in church all I could do is cry uncontrollably. I am sure my friends didn't know how to help me or even know what to say. I took some time to spend with my spiritual mother Mom Brown. I can always be open and honest with her without her judging anything I may say to her.

She began to share with me some personal things about she and her mom. She talked about boundaries and how I had to learn to control our conversation. She asked me, if anything happened to my mother, would I be at peace without talking to her? I lied and said yes. But deep in my heart it would have killed me. The truth is, I was so confused about my emotions, I wanted her to see what she did to me and how wrong she was. I needed to be right. A few weeks later, I had a conversation with another sister-friend. She asked me why I was expecting a 70-year-old woman to change, without thinking that maybe she didn't know how to change. She then reminded me about what I said to her about forgiveness. She shared with me a story about her father who would make her have oral sex with her as a child after church. "If I can forgive him for doing that to me, then you can forgive her." She said to me, "Your problems are never as big as you may think when you hear another person's problems."

I could not deny her words. She spoke truth to my spirit. I knew she was correct. I also knew she loved her father but she also had boundaries. I prayed about it and asked God to show Himself to me and grant me this one thing. I needed a sign from God that He heard me. The next week it was my birthday, June the 20th. The first call that morning, as always, was from my mother. It was as if nothing was wrong, and I was fine with that. From that day on, boundaries with she and I were in place. I also knew my mother was getting old and a major shift was coming. I would not be prepared for what was about to happen.

October 30, 2017

I was at work preparing for a training dinner when my phone rang from an unknown number in D.C. It was Washington Hospital Center calling me to inform me that my mother was there and things were not looking so good for her. I was in shock because I had just spoken to her and she had not mentioned anything to me about her not feeling well. They told me that she had come in because of an infection in her mouth that they later learned was an abscess. When they did more testing on her, they found that her heart was failing her. She also had a really bad kidney infection, and she was showing signs of dementia at a rapid pace. I told them to continue to treat her and keep me posted. I was not aware of half of the things that they were talking to me about, so I reached out to a few nurses I knew to explain to me what was going on. Because I was not with her and we had been in this place before, I was hoping things would turn around for her quickly. Little did I know, things would not turn around at all.

November 6, 2017

Things were getting better up until this point. We found a nursing home to take her to until she was ready to come home. As they were moving her to the home, her heart crashed, so they had to keep her in the hospital for more treatment. We later found out that she had a lung infection and things were starting to take a dive downhill for her. She also was now dealing with her dementia at an alarming rate. When the doctor asked me if I wanted them to resuscitate her or not, I broke down and told him I could not answer that right now. I was not ready to allow myself to think about my mother not being with me. I had no idea what was coming, but I felt a change coming and I was not happy about it.

November 7, 2017

None of the meds were working and her body was shutting down quickly. I knew I had to move fast and there was no time to waste. I had no idea how I was going to get home but I knew I had to go. I called my boss and told him that I needed to go home because my mom was not doing well and I was buying a one-way ticket until whatever happens happens. He told me he would buy the ticket for me and to go take care of my Queen. My prayer was, whatever God's will is for her life. This gave me comfort knowing that God was in control of what was about to happen. I knew she would not like to be connected with tubes or on life support. She always made it very clear she did not like that. Before I went, I had to follow my mother's wishes, so I made the most painful phone call ever. I had to tell her doctors to remove all tubes and do not resuscitate her. That was one of the hardest things I have ever had to say in my life at the time. I would have to say it and hold back my tears.

November 10, 2017

When I got to the hospital, my mother was asleep. The staff at the hospital was waiting for me to come in to update me on what was to come and what to be ready for. I was in one meeting after another. I spent time with her wishing she would wake up and say something to me. When she did open her eyes, she gave me a look that told me she was glad to see me. I got down on the floor next to her bed and kissed her, loving on her and letting her know that I was not going anywhere. She gave me a nod of agreement when I asked her personal questions. I then took her hand and prayed with her. When I was done, she motioned her lips with Amen. I would not let go of her hand. It was a sign to show her I was keeping my word. When she could, she would grip my hand. That was all I needed from her. It was a sign that we were in it together.

November 11, 2017

The staff wanted me to understand what comfort care was, so they sat me down to tell me that, in so many words, my mother was dying. While they were speaking to me, my insides were screaming in pain and I was hurting. It was a feeling I never had before. I could not put my words together or cry in front of people. I knew I had to stay strong for everyone else around me because, in my mind, if I break, then they would break. After the doctors told me about my choices to move her, they gave me paperwork to fill out. I just could not bring myself to signing them, so I waited and prayed about it over the weekend. I was trying to find the inner peace while I watched my mom fight for her time she had on earth. I decided that I was going to celebrate our time together and not rush anything. The time we had was not about me or her. It was about her transition with God and my time with her to honor her. We were in agreement in my spirit and it stayed that way until God was ready for her to come home.

November 12, 2017

It was a Sunday, and for most of the day, it was just she and I. People were in and out to see her, but for the most part, we just looked at each other. As I was about to leave, one of the ministers from her church who she was very fond of came in the room, Reverend Wright. I asked her did she know who he was, and she gave me a sign of yes. He knelt down to her bedside and spoke to her, and she smiled with a big warm look in her eyes and then we prayed. While holding her hand, I noticed she was rubbing my hand with her thumb. I told her to get some rest and I would be back in the morning. She gave me a sign of okay. It was nice to talk with him and allow him to talk. He helped me keep my focus and not sink into depression. He saved me and he didn't even know it.

November 13, 2017

My visit with my mother this day was very different in many ways. On this day she was very alert to everything in the room and to who was coming in and out. A physical therapist came in and she was working with her following all of her commands. She still was not eating anything but she was able to let me know she wanted something to drink. It was as if she needed to clear her throat. As I was holding her hand, she kept looking at me very intensely. She kept moaning something to me and I finally understood. She was saying, "Mama. Mama." She was trying to tell me her mother was in the room. As I was holding her hand reading to her, she gripped my hand and tried to sit up. As I was helping her to do so, she said it. "I LOVE YOU." It was clear and it was as if it took all the strength she had. I said I love you back to her. I then asked her was she scared. She shook her head no, and then she went to sleep. In that moment I felt her strength and her love. I stepped out of the room and wept openly. I knew it would not be long. The next few days all she did was sleep

November 17, 2017

We moved her to Stoddard Baptist Nursing Home. I went to her home and got photos and a blanket she liked, along with other things she used. I was hoping she would wake up and see them and smile. I was in one meeting after another. The staff was very kind but they wanted me to know that this was comfort care. It was their way of telling me that she didn't have long. All I could do was look at her, telling myself to never forget what she looked like. Every now and then she would make a sound but she would not eat. All she wanted to do was sleep. She had been sleeping for the last few days non-stop. It seemed like she was fighting to get some rest, so I let her rest. In the middle of the night she had some major heart issues and was taken to the nearest hospital for treatment. Every time my phone rang, I got knots in my stomach. I wanted her to keep fighting.

November 19, 2017

Mother is taken to Howard Hospital. When I got there she had tubes everywhere and they had mittens on her hands to stop her from pulling them out. She looked so uncomfortable, and I could see that she wanted none of those things on her. I called a meeting with the doctor to tell him her wishes. He gave me paperwork to sign, and they began to remove the tubes. My sister Yevette was in the room with us, and we began to pray and sing songs of worship. I was holding her head and kept saying my name over and over to her with the hopes that she could hear me. It seemed to me she was understanding, and she calmed down and went back to her restful sleep. I was at peace for what was to come for her. My drive back to my friend's home where I was staying was filled with memories of our time as mother and son.

November 20, 2017

Mother was taken back to the nursing home the following day. The next few days she was still not eating and she continued sleeping. I was trying to wrap my head around all this so that I could understand what my lesson was, and then I got it. I had to build my faith and to have courage to grow in all this while in pain. I kept feeling like after this, my life would make a turn that even I was not ready for. I had often spoken openly about my fear of death and how I wanted nothing to do with watching anyone suffer. This was peace. There was no suffering for my mother, and that gave me joy. My spiritual growth and awareness was on high alert. I was sure about what God was saying to me. This was a part of my journey and I was to receive everything that was happening around me as a teaching tool for someone else who would not have the same grace given to them. This was more than life or death. This was spirit connecting to the ultimate Spirit. God was telling me that this moment should be my way of showing God thanks for allowing me to come through the gift in the form of Ruth F. Eubanks. During this entire time, I was praying for God's will to be done and that peace would rule in this transition.

November 24, 2017 at 8:45 am

I had gotten up that morning and sat at the side of the bed feeling like my mother's presence was with me. As I stood up to get dressed to go see my mother at the nursing home, I got a tight feeling in my stomach. Before I made it to the bathroom, the phone rang. I knew in my gut what the call was about, so I took a deep breath and said, "Hello." It was the nursing home calling me to tell me that my mother had transitioned in her sleep that morning. I sat back down and looked out the window and cried for my loss. Then I thanked God for my Angel who would personally watch over me for the rest of my life. In that moment, my life changed forever, and I have never gotten back to that normal way of living since. The night before while eating Thanksgiving dinner, my best friend Kevin said that on his birthday every year it seemed like someone died. In my mind, I felt like God was using him to speak to me. So I prepared myself for what was to come. I think God was telling him that November 24th would be her day of final rest. No matter how much you try to prepare yourself for death, it still hurts like hell. The next few days would be a blur to me. I could not believe my mother was gone.

December 5, 2017

I buried Mother in a purple African suit with gold trimmings with a head wrap to match what she had on, and an African necklace that matched her outfit. She looked so peaceful, almost like she was asleep. Her casket was white with gold trimmings around it. It was called the Virgo, which was also her zodiac sign. Instead of flowers, I had her casket covered with an African fabric I found in this African gift shop in Baltimore. It was a celebration fit for a Queen with music from the choir she had been a part of, laughter about her feistiness, and tears of sadness for our loss. Over a hundred family, church family, life-long friends, and her neighbors all came out in attendance to send her off. Dr. Willie F. Wilson, her Pastor for over forty years, spoke about her dedication of years of service at Union Temple. His message was entitled, "Yet, but not yet." There yet remains a rest for the people of God.

He spoke from out of the book of Hebrews. He spoke about resting in the will of God when your time of service is done on earth. I prepared a message for her and kept changing it. I have no idea what I said that day. It just came out. How I got through any of it was amazing to me. I do know I spoke from my heart, and my purpose was to honor her the best way I knew how, with Love. Her best friend Val and the dance group she was in for over ten years spoke. At the grave site I could not keep it together. The idea that I was never going to see her again hit me. For the next three months I cried and grieved for my loss. My mother's dream in life was to be a writer. It was one of the greatest seeds she gave me. I am honored to carry the torch for her and to live out her dreams through me. Living life one step at a time came from her example of not rushing anything in life. I love how she marched to life in her own rhythm. She would always tell me, "Be the best you you can be. And what you can't do, allow God to do the rest." My goal is to continue to learn the lessons that are for me and to embrace what God has purposed for me. But most importantly, I want to live out loud daily. Because of the seed my mother planted in me, I get to bear the fruit, and I am honored by that.

For speaking engagements for Paul please email him at learning2walk@outlook.com.

Paul Earl Eubanks is a man after God's heart, and he chooses to live his life on assignment for the Kingdom of God. He is a native of Washington, D.C., A Minister, A Teacher, A life coach, A Motivational speaker, A son, and now An Author. Paul is bold and unashamed of his testimony. He has built an extensive faith resume through actively searching the Word of God and applying its truths over his circumstances in prayer and the willingness to make the necessary changes for growth. Paul's own heart is one of loyalty and service. He capitalizes on each opportunity to minister healing in any setting you may find him. The addicted, the homeless, and the sick are just a few of those who have received his message of hope and wholeness. Learning 2 Walk Again is his most personal ministry yet.

Printed in the United States
By Bookmasters